PARADISE LOST
as "MYTH"

PARADISE LOST
as "MYTH"

Isabel Gamble MacCaffrey

HARVARD UNIVERSITY PRESS

Cambridge, Massachusetts

1 9 6 7

Second printing

Distributed in Great Britain by Oxford University Press, London

The publication of this book has been aided by a grant
from the Ford Foundation

Library of Congress Catalog Card Number 59-9282
Printed in the United States of America

TO

ELIZABETH COX WRIGHT

AND

EVERETT HUNT

PREFATORY NOTE

Some of my debts are longstanding, beginning with those acknowledged in the dedication. At an early stage I was able to spend a year in England on a Fulbright fellowship, where my first gropings toward this book were sympathetically assisted by Miss M. G. Lloyd Thomas, of Girton College, Cambridge. Several members of the Department of English of Harvard University provided helpful comments; two must be specially mentioned. Herschel Baker read the manuscript when it was young and offered encouragement that cheered the labors of a weary graduate student and illuminated her path. My greatest debt is to Douglas Bush, under whose supervision the first version of this book saw the light. He endured patiently the vagaries of my proceedings, tamed a proud pretending wit, and with kind scholarly firmness curbed the wilder flights of an unschooled imagination. That some evaded his control cannot reflect on him, but only proves once more how obstinacy resists true wisdom, how "apt the Mind or Fancie is to roave."

Finally, my husband has provided support, moral, intellectual, and economic, all with equal generosity and with unfailing amiability.

Isabel Gamble MacCaffrey

Bryn Mawr College
October 1958

CONTENTS

ELH	*A Journal of English Literary History*
ESEA	*Essays and Studies by Members of the English Association*
HTR	*Harvard Theological Review*
JEGP	*Journal of English and Germanic Philology*
JHI	*Journal of the History of Ideas*
MLN	*Modern Language Notes*
MP	*Modern Philology*
PMLA	*Publications of the Modern Language Association of America*
PQ	*Philological Quarterly*
RES	*Review of English Studies*
SP	*Studies in Philology*
UTQ	*University of Toronto Quarterly*

INTRODUCTION

The purpose of this book is to conduct a literary investigation of a particular kind, for which *Paradise Lost* provides the impetus, occasion, and experimental field. The aim is to make a descriptive analysis of Milton's poem; and this phrase is chosen deliberately as a limiting one. On one hand, "analysis" excludes purely historical considerations except as they may be relevant to an overriding purpose; on the other, "descriptive" disclaims polemics. I have not been especially concerned with Milton's "life and thought"; that concern has already produced studies of great value by others. Nor shall I justify the ways of Milton in poetry, unless a demonstration of how some special problems were effectively solved by him, can be called justification. The enduring value of *Paradise Lost,* its claim not merely as an historical document, but as a work of art, on our continuing interest, is assumed, not argued. I have hoped, in short, that the book would serve the first two functions of criticism as T. S. Eliot has named them: analysis and elucidation. The third, comparison, and a putative fourth, judgment, are not part of the current undertaking, though not because I consider them unworthy or superfluous.

I do not intend to argue, either, the question of how far Milton was, or was not, the inventor of the ideas he chose to treat. It is clear at once to any informed reader of *Paradise*

1

Lost that Milton's subject matter cannot be "original" except in the literal sense that it deals with origins. Insofar as the poem is Christian, its themes are the themes of Christian thought from earliest times; insofar as Christianity incorporated still more ancient traditions, its themes are those of the immemorial human imagination; and since it was written in the seventeenth century, the idiom of its ideas can be linked at many points to that of the age. The uniqueness of *Paradise Lost* is in a sense its perfect victory over uniqueness; the very thoroughness with which Milton has assimilated the themes relevant to his great story gives it a special place in poetry as the definitive statement of its subject. On the other hand, the poem has obviously the formal originality of every successful work of art, to which the technical apparatus of epic precedent contributes, without impugning. *Paradise Lost* does not sound like any other poem — we can identify its note from the briefest random quotation; nor is it constructed like any other — only Dante matches Milton in architectural power applied to protean material, and he used a quite different blueprint.

Confronted by an enormous work like Milton's epic, the critic must find a way in that will be definite enough to give his examination focus, and at the same time close enough to the central issues of the poem to compass the important unities beneath its variety. I have hoped to achieve this double end by invoking the concept of "myth," not without misgivings, and in the knowledge that a degree of prior explanation would be required. A great deal of scholarly and critical attention has been devoted to Milton over the last few decades; in the process, "Milton's myth" has become a phrase acceptable, even commonplace, in referring to the subject matter of *Paradise Lost*. Acceptable, but ambiguous; for one is seldom sure of the implication that *myth* is meant to carry.

It may be a portentous synonym for the plot — what the eighteenth century called the fable; it is sometimes a covert way of suggesting that the writer does not agree with the doctrine expressed in the poem. I have tried, therefore, to give the word a more precise content than it usually bears in literary discussion, in the hope that it may be a viable concept when a definition of the sort of poem Milton wrote is attempted. This exposition occupies Chapter I, briefly; I have resisted the temptation to ramble in the enchanted forest of mythology, though anyone familiar with the terrain will recognize landmarks set up by worthier predecessors. Like most enchanted woods, it is full of Dens of Error and paths leading nowhere, especially dangerous for the amateur. I have paused only long enough, therefore, to indicate those elements of myth that may prepare us to accept its usefulness as a tool in reading Milton's poem, including under "usefulness" particularly the ways in which a mythical subject might affect the formal qualities of poetry. Nothing will be said about a number of technical problems that have exercised specialists; on questions like the origins of myth I am not competent to pronounce, and they cannot in any case affect the answers we give to critical queries.

Like all critical gambits, this one excludes certain possibilities even as it opens up others. There is much more to be said, and from many other points of view, about the matters considered here; for instance, the language of *Paradise Lost* deserves a book to itself (which it has not yet been given), and a single short chapter will appear sketchy and foreshortened. On the other hand, consideration of the poem as myth may unexpectedly illuminate some befogged areas of Milton criticism. It suggests, for example, one reason why Milton was a peculiarly unsuitable model for imitation by other poets, having designed his epic to answer the needs of

Is it any funxuing the last word in your subject?

a subject that was losing its validity for poetry even as he wrote. It is, indeed, difficult to think of any period since 1667 that could find in *Paradise Lost* a useful technical precedent; when the myth, as Milton understood it, became irrelevant to the world's convictions, the poetic manner created to embody it became obsolete, or, vainly applied to non-mythical subjects, extraneous and dead. In one sense, therefore, it is perfectly true that Milton represents the end of a tradition rather than the "main stream" of future English poetry. New forms of thought arose to make new demands on poetic resources, which had to be answered in new ways. Milton's *technical* lesson for us now is not in the particular poetic devices of *Paradise Lost,* but in his example as a conscientious artist: we are to think of him as the grand creator and preserver of decorum — a supreme poetic virtue, called today by other names — on a scale scarcely matched in English, once we have spoken of Shakespeare.

Paradise Lost is to be read as a work of art, where form and theme are as intimately related as an arc's convex and concave. The precise nature of the relationship, like the mind-body problem, is a tangle of speculation that "ravels more, still less resolved," the more it is handled. Quarrels about terminology perplex it; or the knot is cut by declaring the problem to be a pseudo-problem. The very names of "form" and "content" are denounced as violations of essential unity. Bypassing treatises on aesthetics, one makes do with whatever formulas will temporarily work. In saying, then, that the form of *Paradise Lost* was dictated by its subject, I am not making judgments about the temporal priority of "subject" in the creative process, though the theme of the epic, in its broadest sense, was present in Milton's mind from his youth. Like any other poetic subject, this myth implied, required, or depended upon certain formal necessities. The writings of Ernst Cassirer, among others, have accustomed us to considering myth as "a *form* of thought." [1] The myths of man's origin and destiny that compose the fable of *Paradise Lost* involved a certain "manner of seeing" which in turn tended to produce a particular kind of formal shape in any discourse based on them. In designing his poem, Milton was the master, not the slave, of formal literary precedents; he was, above all, fulfilling by the most suitable means he could contrive, the demands of his subject. The result is a work at once traditional and profoundly new.

An outline of Milton's mythic themes in the second chapter concludes, therefore, with some discussion of the way in which they can most suitably be treated in poetry. In spite of Milton's declaration of aim, to justify the ways of God to men, the undertaking did not proceed discursively, as the word *justify* commonly leads us to expect. In *Paradise Lost* we are given, not primarily thoughts, but the *content* of thoughts about God's ways: images, not ideas. R. P. Blackmur has said, "Thought requires of us that we make a form for our knowledge which is personal, declarative, and abstract at the same time that we construe it as impersonal, expressive, and concrete." [2] Milton fulfilled the requirements of thought elsewhere; in *Paradise Lost,* he went beyond these requirements to achieve the impersonal, expressive, and concrete construing of ultimate experience. It will be well to keep Blackmur's terms in mind, since all three are directly pertinent to the "lawless" and unique style developed by Milton out of the pressures of his subject.

[1] The title and subject of Part I of *Mythical Thought,* ed. Charles W. Hendel, trans. R. Manheim (New Haven, 1955). This volume is the second of Cassirer's three-volume work collectively titled *The Philosophy of Symbolic Forms.*

[2] "The Expense of Greatness," *The Lion and the Honeycomb* (London, 1956), p. 95.

Such theoretical concerns are introductory to the book's main business, to which the remaining chapters are devoted: a study, in what might be called eclectic detail, of the techniques that enforce Milton's themes in poetry. The interlocking structure of *Paradise Lost,* carried by patterns of verbal and imagistic echoes as well as by a careful architectural plan, has been stressed, and this has required a good deal of motif-tracing, with its inevitable repetitions. Milton's methods in this poem are on the whole straightforward and iterative rather than ambiguous and inventive; one finds the same "idea" expressed often in a number of different ways, and the instruments of expression are many, large and small: a book or group of books, a scene, a landscape, an adjective.

There remain one or two possible misunderstandings to be forestalled. The problem of an author's "intention" has lately received some scrutiny from writers on aesthetics, who conclude that it has very little relevance for the critic, if by intention we understand a clear-cut, completed meaning which the author sets out to enshrine in a work of art.[3] The evident falsity of this concept when applied to much creative activity does not, however, render it completely useless as a critical tool; every intellectual operation proceeds from a more or less makeshift convention. And intention obviously *may* have a meaning at one stage of any writing: in the choice of genre, a kind of intention is manifested, often explicitly, always with a degree of deliberation. An author must know whether he is setting out to write an epic or a lyric, a novel in hundreds of pages or a short story in a score. Milton's enumeration of available genres in *The*

[3] The occasion for the discussion, and key essay, is M. C. Beardsley and W. K. Wimsatt, "The Intentional Fallacy," *Sewanee Review,* LIV (1946), 468–88. It has since been reprinted in Wimsatt's collection of essays, *Verbal Icon* (University of Kentucky [Lexington], 1954).

Reason of Church Government documents this stage for his
own career. The writer, in choosing to work in one literary
form, is at the same time fixing his theme, or at least com-
mitting himself to a particular sort of emphasis. As every
seventeenth-century poet knew, there is a <u>generic decorum</u>,
not only of style but of subject, "which is the grand master-
piece to observe." The interdependence of form and content
holds for literary types as well as single works. One can
think of short stories, or lyrics, or novels, in which there
is a dissonance between the chosen form and the task it is
employed to accomplish; realization of the theme is incomplete because the technique is too feeble to encompass
it, or redundant because the machinery is too massive for
the material. And there are other kinds of disproportion,
more subtle than size. Occasionally, we can observe a theme
being foreshortened, altered, or actually transformed under
the pressure of the form; again, the formal intention may
contract or expand as the nature of the theme is gradually
revealed as more or less complex or intense.

Beyond this point, however, a discussion of "intention"
is not likely to be profitable. Even the statements of purpose
left by Milton, who was unusually articulate in these matters,
do not take us very far toward a comprehension of *Paradise
Lost*. Other critical tools are needed, and they will be drawn
inevitably from the critic's own intellectual background, a
necessity deplored by the historical isolationist who fears
that the poetic object, itself the product of a unique milieu,
will be distorted beyond recognition by relating it to
methods and ideas alien in time and purpose. Too much
can be made of supposed violations of historical realism,
though the dutiful critic will of course read as far as possible
in the same spirit as the author writ. But that possibility is
limited. William James called pragmatism a new name for

I am not sure I know what is being said

some old ways of thinking, and at its best the criticism of every age, interpreting the past anew, sees the same objects but calls them by new names. One can remain faithful to Milton's poetic concerns without being obliged to use only a vocabulary that he would have recognized. "I gotta use words when I talk to you" — but what words? The contemporary dialect must serve. Thus every work will be reinterpreted freshly in each generation; metempsychosis becomes a necessary part of every critic's private credo as he sees the labors of his predecessors made obsolete by those of his contemporaries.

It is, finally, unimportant whether or not we "like" a particular terminology, or accept as "true" a scaffolding of ideas which by its nature must have a limited validity. The test is pragmatic: does it work, does it further analysis and elucidation? What matters is poems (novels, plays) and their accessibility. Their voices do not cease; it is for us to tune our ears as best we can.

I

THE MEANING OF "MYTH"

In the discussion of myth, as in more august undertakings, the first step is the hardest. We must disburden the word itself of the weighty irrelevant associations that have gathered round to deform it in the generations since it became current in English. The first entry of a related word in the *New English Dictionary* gives the clue for one group of emotive meanings: "Mythic, or Fabulous, Theologie, at first broached by the Poets." [1] Fabulous; *ergo,* a fable, false. More than two hundred years later, an echo is heard from Sir James Frazer, perhaps the most successful agent of the revived popular interest in myth that occurred at the beginning of this century. "By myths I understand mistaken explanations of phenomena, whether of human life or of external nature." [2] The idea of a myth as something that no enlightened person could possibly believe is by now indelibly fixed in "usage"; one cannot hope to eradicate statements like "The unicorn is a mythical beast." James

1 John Gale, *Court of the Gentiles* (1669), *NED*, s.v. "mythic."
2 Introduction to Apollodorus' *Library*, Loeb Classical Library (2 vols., London & New York, 1921), I, xxvii.

9

Thurber's moral tale is instructive, however; the unicorn, though mythical, was really in the garden, and ate the roses.

On the other hand, a counter-group of implications has recently accumulated around *myth,* honorific rather than pejorative. Myth is defined as the constant element of value in the products of human civilization, particularly in religion and literature. It signifies a mode of experience archaic but still somehow relevant, speaking from, or to, deep-seated responses in the human mind. The events of mythology, it is claimed, "remain ageless, inexhaustible, invincible in timeless primordiality, in a past that proves imperishable because of its eternally repeated rebirths." [3] A closer look at these latter-day refurbishments of myth discloses, however, a radical error, shared with the earlier writers who dismissed myth as "Fabulous Theologie." Both views seek to impose alien standards of "reality" or importance, ignoring the attitudes of the believers to whom the myths originally belonged, who had inherited, lived with, and loved or feared them. The seventeenth-century commentator considered "mythic" tales to be merely false; for Frazer and most of his contemporaries, they were again false, though well-intentioned and serious. For present-day writers, myths are usually taken to "mean" something important, but they are still thought of as being *in themselves* — uninterpreted — "fabulous" or even nonsensical. [4]

Nineteenth-century anthropologists "explained" myth in varying and often mutually exclusive terms: the myth was

[3] Carl Gustav Jung and Károly Kerényi, *Introduction to a Science of Mythology* (London, 1950), p. 9.

[4] Witness the common practice of lumping together myths and dreams in psychological discussions, e.g., by Erich Fromm: "All myths and all dreams have one thing in common, they are all 'written' in the same language, *symbolic language.*" *The Forgotten Language* (New York, 1951), p. 7.

an early type of scientific theory, "a disease of language," a dim groping after philosophical truth, or a garbled version of historical events; in short, a "mistaken" statement of facts about the outside world. Contemporary psychology looks on myth as a veiled statement of facts about the interior world, in which psychological events are enacted as a story. All these writers insist on *analysis* in terms other than those provided by the myths themselves. "They hope to make us understand the mythical world by a process of intellectual reduction." [5] This position has been given a useful formulation by Jung: "What an archetypal content [that is, myth or dream] is always expressing is first and foremost a *figure of speech.*" [6] The myth becomes a vehicle for which the tenor must be supplied by the interpreter; and while interpreters may differ in the direction of their aim, they agree on the target. The original story is left behind as a sort of husk from which the kernel of meaning has been successfully retrieved.

At the root of all the attitudes described above is a single fact: the inability of any of the commentators to believe that mythical stories are, or were, *true,* in any recognizable sense of the word. This inability was shared up to a point by Milton and his contemporaries, who clearly did not "believe" the tales they read in Hesiod, Herodotus, Ovid, Plutarch, or more exotic purveyors of the wisdom of the ancients. Bacon's allegorical interpretations in *De sapientia veterum* are, indeed, often as tortuously ingenious as any propounded by a modern Jungian. The mythographers of the Renaissance, however, tended to see myth in terms not of metaphor, but of *mimesis.* The myths of other cultures reflected, dimly and in distorted outline, larger more porten-

---

[5] Ernst Cassirer, *An Essay on Man* (New Haven, 1944), p. 75.
[6] Jung and Kerényi, *Introduction,* p. 105.

tous figures. They were, in Ralegh's pregnant phrase, "crooked images of some one true history."[7] The nature of that *one* was never in doubt; it was the Christian version of human destiny. Ralegh elaborates his point in a cautious paragraph.

The occasion offereth itself for us to consider, how the Greeks and other more ancient nations, by fabulous inventions, and by breaking into parts the story of the creation, and by delivering it over in a mystical sense, wrapping it up mixed with other their own trumpery, have sought to obscure the truth thereof. . . . But as a skilful and learned chymist can as well by separation of visible elements draw helpful medicines out of poison, as poison out of the most healthful herbs and plants . . . so, contrary to the purposes and hopes of the heathen, may those who seek after God and truth find out every where, and in all the ancient poets and philosophers, the story of the first age, with all the works and marvels thereof, amply and lively expressed.[8]

His belief "that in old corruptions we may find some signs of more ancient truth" was stated and restated often in the years before Milton wrote *Paradise Lost.* Bacon was less specific, but as insistent, in announcing that myths must be regarded "as sacred relics and light airs breathing out of better times, that were caught from the traditions of more ancient nations and so received into the flutes and trumpets of the Greeks."[9]

Such interpretations, dwelling on Greek trumpets, or trumpery, continued well into the seventeenth century. Giles Fletcher provided a poetic link between "the obscure fables of the Gentiles" and the images of Biblical history.

---

[7] Sir Walter Ralegh, *The History of the World, Works,* ed. William Oldys and Thomas Birch (8 vols., Oxford, 1829), II, 176.

[8] *Works,* II, 163.

[9] *De sapientia veterum, Works,* ed. James Spedding, Robert Leslie Ellis, and Douglas Denon Heath (14 vols., London, 1878), VI, 698.

Who doth not seen drown'd in Deucalions name,
(When earth his men, and sea had lost his shore)
Old Noah; and in Nisus lock, the fame
Of Sampson yet alive; and long before
In Phaethons, mine owne fall I deplore:
  But he that conquer'd hell, to fetch againe
  His virgin widowe, by a serpent slaine,
Another Orpheus was then dreaming poets feigne.[10]

Themes closer to Milton's are worried by his contemporary Henry Reynolds who, assuming that the ancients concealed important truths under "riddles and enigmaticall knotts," busied himself in finding parallels between "the sacred letter and Ethnick Poesyes." In *Mythomystes* (1632), he poses some rhetorical questions:

What could they meane by their *Golden-Age, . . .* but the state of Man before his Sin? and consequently, by their Iron age, but the worlds infelicity and miseries that succeeded his fall? . . . Lastly . . . what can *Adonis horti* among the Poets meane other then *Moses* his *Eden,* or terresiall Paradise?

There follows some learned talk about word derivations, concluding with a discussion of the Latin *Paradisus* or Eden, "the which selfe thing the auncient both Poets and Philosophers certainely ment by their *horti Hesperidum* likewise." [11] A final example, certainly familiar to Milton, from Sylvester's translation of DuBartas, unmasks the dark pagan conspiracy as the model of the "true" Eden is unveiled in verse.

    Ye Pagan Poets that audaciously
    Have sought to dark the ever-Memory

---

[10] *Christs Victorie and Triumph, The Poetical Works of Giles and Phineas Fletcher,* ed. F. S. Boas (2 vols., Cambridge, 1908), I, 59.

[11] *Critical Essays of the Seventeenth Century,* ed. J. E. Spingarn (3 vols., Oxford, 1908–1909), I, 156, 175–76.

> Of God's great Works; from henceforth still be dum
> Your fabled prayses of *Elysium;*
> Which by this goodly Module you have wrought,
> Through deaf tradition, that your Fathers taught:
> For, the Almighty made his blissfull bowrs
> Better indeed then you have fained yours.[12]

Indeed, the opinion of Reynolds and Sylvester, of Bacon and
Fletcher, was too familiar and widespread in this period to
require further illustration. Dante had put the point more
shortly when, in the real Earthly Paradise, he recalled the
crooked images of that garden in the poets' reminiscences
of a Golden Age:

> Quelli che anticamente poetaro
>   l'eta dell' oro e suo stato felice,
>   forse in Parnaso esto loco sognaro.[13]

The attitude of all these earlier writers toward myth must
be carefully distinguished from modern interpretations. For
us, in general, all myths have the same status; typically, the
"Christian myth" is read as a version of a story well known
to other cultures, and Christ becomes one among many
dying gods. For the Renaissance, all myths are reflections,
distorted or mutilated though they may be, of the "one true
history," which differs from them ontologically. It is the
source, the one root from which many thematic branches
have sprung: the prototype whose ectypes form the multi-
tudinous shapes of history. This relationship will necessarily

---

12 *The Divine Weekes,* Second Week, First Day, Part I; *The Complete
Works of Joshua Sylvester,* ed. A. B. Grosart (2 vols., Edinburgh, 1880), I,
100.

13 "They who in olden times sang of the golden age and its happy state,
perchance dreamed in Parnassus of this place." *Purgatorio,* xxviii. 139–141.
Translated by Thomas Okey. The Temple Classics (London, 1946), pp.
356–57.

prevail in an age of belief where there is, at the same time, a sense of history. The attempt of Pico della Mirandola to reconcile not only Plato and Aristotle, but the truths hidden in all religions, with Christianity, reflects the natural impulse of a period at once learned, eclectic, and powerfully religious.

In fact, of course, every myth has been treated at some time, by someone, not as make-believe, but as belief.[14] The point of this observation is not to condemn unbelievers, or to cast doubt on "interpretations" of mythical material by psychologists and others, who must serve their own purposes; it is merely to suggest that an examination of what *belief* in myth involved is essential if we are to understand a poem that sets out to embody a myth. For a believer, then, the mythic "fable" is to be taken as the record of a real happening, "one true *history*," and to be read more or less literally. Here is an anthropologist's account:

Myth as it exists in a savage community . . . is not of the nature of fiction, such as we read today in a novel, but it is a living reality, believed to have once happened in primeval times, and continuing ever since to influence the world and human destinies. This myth is to the savage what, to a fully believing Christian, is the Biblical story of Creation, of the Fall, of the Redemption by Christ's Sacrifice on the Cross. . . . Studied alive, myth . . . is not symbolic, but a direct expression of its subject-matter; it is not an explanation in satisfaction of a scientific interest, but a narrative resurrection of a primitive reality, told in satisfaction of deep religious wants.[15]

As "a narrative resurrection of primitive reality," the myth records a prehistoric event from which all later realities

---

[14] Paraphrase of a remark by Cassirer, *Essay on Man*, p. 74.
[15] Bronislaw Malinowski, *Myth in Primitive Psychology* (New York, 1926), pp. 18–19.

in history are descended, and by which they are influenced.[16]
The reality of occurrences in time — "imperishable because of its eternally repeated rebirths" — no longer *depends
on* their recurrent manifestations; rather, their existence
is made to depend on the prior reality of a metaphysical
condition that is their cause. The myth, far from being a
symbolic version of some distant truth, is itself the model of
which everyday reality is in some sense the symbol.

The metaphysical and causal priority of myth may suggest
an analogy that has sometimes been used in this connection:
the Platonic Idea.[17] The Idea and the myth are alike in two
ways; formally, they are both patterns for lesser, subsequent
entities, and existentially, both have real being, independent
of temporal manifestations, and self-sufficient or necessary
as distinct from the contingent reality of their "imitations"
in time. Ralegh's phrase, "crooked images," for pagan tales
as they reflect Christian myth, could apply equally to the
physical objects of the world as they mirror the unchanging
Ideas. In both instances, superior metaphysical qualities are
conferred (or inferred): the Idea, or myth, is *more* "real,"
more "true" than the particulars in which it is darkly reflected. This description echoes the philosophers' attempts
to define God as the First Cause, fully realized being, the
source of truth. With reason; for to a believer in the myth,

[16] According to the "ritual theory," now widely held, this postulated
"causal" relation is reversed to explain the *origin* of myth: a myth may have
been invented to "explain" a set of facts, usually embodied in a ritual, and
may thus be genetically later than its chronological "descendants" in ritual
action. "The myth . . . actually identifies the present, in its ritual aspect,
with a past . . . in which superhuman figures devote themselves to the
performance of acts which are the prototypes of the ritual." Lord Raglan,
The Hero, The Thinker's Library (London, 1949), p. 131.

[17] See Francis Cornford, "A Ritual Basis for Hesiod's *Theogony," The
Unwritten Philosophy and Other Essays,* ed. W. K. C. Guthrie (Cambridge,
1950), p. 111.

the story read by others as a fairy-tale possesses many of the numinous and determinative qualities ascribed in more elaborate religions to the Deity. Studied alive, the myth takes on its original power as the poetic expression of ultimate reality: "it expresses, enhances, and codifies belief." [18]

The terms of Ralegh's formula must, then, be confirmed for this study: the myth is to be read as *true,* and as *history.* It is also, as the third term states, *one;* paradoxically, both unique and universal. Unique, because it reports an event that happened once, and happened actually; universal, because it records events of critical importance. The Fall of Man is the hinge of human fate, and the Sacrifice and Redemption demanded by it are also unique, as St. Paul explains.

For Christ is not entered into the holy places made with hands, which are the figures of the true; but into heaven itself, now to appear in the presence of God for us. . . .
Now once in the end of the world hath he appeared to put away sin by the sacrifice of himself.
And as it is appointed unto men once to die, but after this the judgment:
So Christ was once offered to bear the sins of many.[19]

The repeated word *once* is the key to this passage.

As the myth is unique, so is it universal. Mythical events exert a decisive influence on subsequent history; they are prototypical and explanatory, providing the clue to many like experiences, and their original. Milton, in his Latin poem "On the Platonic Idea as understood by Aristotle," describes the nature of such an "original" image, archetypal man.

18 Malinowski, *Myth in Primitive Psychology,* p. 19.
19 Hebrews, 9:24–28.

Quis ille primus cujus ex imagine
Natura sollers finxit humanum genus,
Aeternus, incorruptus, aequaevus polo,
Unusque et universus, exemplar Dei?

Milton's adjectives for the Idea are significant: *unus et
universus.* He adds,

Sed quamlibet natura sit communior,
Tamen seorsus extat ad morem unius.[20]

This ancestor's nature is general, yet we are to conceive of
him "in the manner of an individual"; it is a forecast of
the Adam of *Paradise Lost.* On him, nature has moulded all
humanity; he is "original" and mythic.

In reading Milton's poem, then, we must accept, however
temporarily, the existence of a "real" supernatural world, and
✓regard the myth as Dr. Johnson regarded the fable when he
read *Paradise Lost:* "It contains the history of a miracle." [21]
As a result, the critical undertaking that follows will be quite
unlike such tracing of mythological "motifs" as can be
found, for example, in the books of Maud Bodkin. The
content of Milton's myth has been studied with scholarly
concentration from the vantage-points of theology, com-

---

[20] "Who was that primal man in whose image cunning Nature fashioned
the human race, a man eternal, incorruptible, of equal age with the sky, at
once single and universal, the model of the Deity? . . . But, although his
nature is quite general, nevertheless he exists apart in the manner of an
individual." *De idea Platonica quemadmodum Aristoteles intellexit,* ll. 7–10,
13–14. Translated by Nelson G. McCrea.

The texts of Milton's poems, including *Paradise Lost,* are taken throughout
from *The Student's Milton,* ed. Frank Allen Patterson, revised edition (New
York, 1933), where the original spelling and punctuation are preserved. The
edition of Helen Darbishire in the Oxford English Texts (2 vols., Oxford,
1952–55), the most recent and meticulous, is less available to the general
student.

[21] Samuel Johnson, *Lives of the English Poets,* ed. G. Birkbeck Hill (3
vols., Oxford, 1905), I, 174.

parative religion, philosophy, psychology, the Renaissance "world-picture," Jungian theory, and so on. The interest here is rather in the *formal* nature of the myth as material for poetry: what is demanded of a poem if it is to maintain decorum with the mythic subject of *Paradise Lost?*

This is not to say that there are not many mythological analogues, or motifs, to be found in Milton's epic. Learned in the rival myths of other cultures, he was well aware of their parallels with the one true history, and he absorbed them deliberately into *Paradise Lost* as reflectors of the main theme. An obvious instance is the much-quoted passage on the "gathering" of Proserpina by gloomy Dis, with its oblique glance at Eve and Satan. It is a useful example for pinning down the precise relation between a developed, believed-in myth and the looser concept of a mythological motif, image, or theme. These are ordinarily distinguished, even though the terminology and definitions vary; for instance, Jung remarks that the images of fantasy and dream "are never (or at least very seldom) myths with a definite form, but rather mythological components which, because of their typical nature, we can call 'motifs,' 'primordial images,' types or . . . archetypes." [22] Not only Jungian archetypes, but most Freudian symbols, fit into the category of "components": tree, ocean, casket, siren, old man, and so on. They are always to be read symbolically, as *standing for* some hidden significance; elaborated into more complex patterns, they form mythological themes that flourish as plot elements in the literature of all periods, variously habited. Most of them will be readily recognized by frequenters of

[22] Jung and Kerényi, *Introduction*, p. 9. A similar distinction is suggestively developed by Jacques Maritain, between what he calls "poetic myth" and "metaphysical myth." The latter includes "the organic signs and symbols of some faith actually lived." *Creative Intuition in Art and Poetry,* Bollingen Series XXXV (New York, 1953), p. 180, n. 33.

modern literary criticism: the Golden Age, the night journey, the violation of innocence (for example, Proserpina and gloomy Dis), the dying and revived god, the waste land redeemed. They appear, too, in *myths* — but raised, as we have seen, to a higher power, and awarded a special convincingness based on a claim to "historical" reality.

The difference between myth and theme in literature will, I hope, emerge more fully as the investigation proceeds. Its nature can be suggested briefly by contrasting Spenser's allegory at the end of *The Faerie Queene,* Book I, with Book VI of *Paradise Lost,* or with *Paradise Regained.* The Red Cross Knight challenges a dragon whose ancestry includes "that old serpent"; the battle itself lasts three days; at the end, after resuscitation from the Fountain of Life, the Knight redeems a "forwasted kingdom" where the parents of lost and exiled Truth live. The analogies with the War in Heaven and the life of Christ are obvious; and yet it is not Christ who does battle here, but the Christian soldier whose life repeats the pattern of his Master's. The Knight is the ectype, Christ the prototype, the original of all later copies. The myths embodied in Milton's poems provide "originals" in a causal as well as a formal sense — for example, of Spenser's nostalgia for a lost age of simplicity. The archetypal event is recorded in Book XI of *Paradise Lost,* when the accents of mourning and homesickness are first heard in Eden.

Must I thus leave thee Paradise? thus leave
Thee Native Soile, these happie Walks and Shades,
Fit haunt of Gods? where I had hope to spend,
Quiet though sad, the respit of that day
That must be mortal to us both. O flours,
That never will in other Climate grow,
My early visitation, and my last
At Eev'n, which I bred up with tender hand

From the first op'ning bud, and gave ye Names,
Who now shall reare ye to the Sun, or ranke
Your Tribes, and water from th' ambrosial Fount? (xi.269–79)

Adam and Eve's descendants are doomed to echo this ancestral lament, as Spenser does in his comparisons between the iron age of his life and an earlier time when "the first blossome of fair vertue" flourished.

The direct use of myth in a poem such as *Paradise Lost,* as distinct from oblique references to it in the mythic incidents of *The Faerie Queene* or *Pilgrim's Progress,* clearly implies a kind of literalness that we are not always prepared to allow a poet. Although Milton, like Spenser and Bunyan, would have laid stress on the "spiritual" significance of his story, and its continuing relevance to our own lives, he would also have insisted, as they would not have done in quite the same way, on the validity of its literal "appearances" as he presented them. In spite of token apologies scattered through the poem ("Thus measuring things in Heav'n by things on Earth"), Milton claimed, not idly, that he was accurately depicting "things invisible to mortal sight," "things unattempted yet in Prose or Rhime." We need not, and cannot, measure precisely the degree of literalness that he meant to confer on each detail of the poem, though a reader of the *Christian Doctrine* will agree that it is greater than casual acquaintance might suggest. What we must recognize is Milton's conviction that, allowing for the inevitable margin of error, he was portraying fact. The claim for the truth of events is absolute: these things happened; for the truth of images — the poem's places and personages — less absolute, but still insistent that the qualities and potencies bodied forth in them are real.

Changeless mythological themes which can fit into a variety of contexts and be adapted to multiple meanings are, no

doubt, more fundamental to the human psyche than theology; they are, nevertheless, particularized and made concrete according to the individual's convictions. Faced with
competing mythical explanations, he must decide which is
to be the theme and which the variations. The supreme
validity of his own fable, the unequal status of rival myths,
were fundamental principles for Milton, and must remain
so for us if we are to read *Paradise Lost* properly. While
never denying the richness of symbolic meanings in the
story of the Garden, he shared the Augustinian view that
"these and suchlike [interpretations] may be lawfully understood by paradise, taken in a spiritual sense, provided that
the history of the true local one be as firmly believed." [23]
History, true, local: Augustine insists that the myth be understood, and recorded, on a primary level of belief before it can
be "interpreted." Milton set out in *Paradise Lost* to embody
the history of the true local Garden; from the contemplation
of this unique piece of history was to be deduced a justification of God's ways. The poem *itself* is not justification, but
presentation, and the conditions of that presentation are
now to be explored.

[23] St. Augustine, *The City of God*, trans. John Healey, Everyman's Library
(2 vols., London, 1945), Book XIII, ch. 22; II, 18.

II

MILTON'S MYTH

THE CHRISTIAN PARADIGM

Students of comparative mythology have often attempted to establish a [paradigm] to which all local myths could be *model or pattern* related as instances. These efforts are alike chiefly in their sketchiness and dogmatism, and their results are not usually helpful, since a comprehensive scheme will necessarily turn out to be so elastic that no product of the human imagination need fall outside it. There is, however, rough agreement that a threefold pattern, following a cyclical or spiral path, is common to very many myths. Joseph Campbell connects this scheme with "the formula represented in the rites of passage: *separation — initiation — return:* which might be called the nuclear unit of the monomyth." [1] *Return* is a vital thread in the pattern. The mythic journey of life is circular; it leads around the world, or back to the starting-point, until we catch sight of the immortal sea that brought us hither. As Milton had it:

After wandering about upon the earth for some time, like some heavenly visitant, in holiness and righteousness, [man's] spirit

[1] *The Hero with a Thousand Faces* (New York, 1949), p. 30.

23

was to take its flight upward to the heaven whence it had come and to return once more to the abode and home which was its birthright.[2]

Although this destiny was marred and made uncertain by the Fall of Man, the memory of it remains in the midst of our present wanderings, to urge the soul upward; for the Christian, nostalgia and hope live side by side.

The Adam who leaves Paradise to wander down to a lower world is a wayfarer, and will always be, until the end returns him to his beginning. He is, besides, a warrior who must do battle with a monster within himself in order to complete his journey — and the father of a long line of heroes who will face in each generation a reincarnation of the old Serpent. Adam, the meek but steadfast Christian soldier, is "to overcom By suffering, and earne rest from labour won" (xi.375–76). Milton's subject in *Paradise Lost* is the necessity by which man became both a wayfaring and a warfaring Christian.[3]

The metaphor of human life as a warfare, and as a "wandering" or pilgrimage, provided plot and imagery for innumerable literary and devotional works from the Middle Ages, with the *Pélerinage de la vie humaine* as a prototype, on into the Renaissance. Ralegh, recounting the beginning of human time in his *History,* quoted Bede:

For eating the forbidden fruit of the tree of knowledge was Adam driven out of Paradise, *in exilium vitae temporalis,* "into the banishment of temporal life," saith Beda.[4]

The exile of our life, occasioned by the Fall, was the second

2 Prolusion VII, *Private Correspondence and Academic Exercises,* trans. P. B. Tillyard, ed. E. M. W. Tillyard (Cambridge, 1932), p. 107.

3 For the variant reading of Milton's phrase in *Areopagitica,* "the true warfaring Christian," see *The Student's Milton,* Notes, p. 114.

4 *Works,* II, 129.

stage of the Christian drama, following the brief idyl of the Garden. It led, in hope, to the third: recovery of lost paradise, the past recaptured, the wound healed. Everyman, heir of the fallen Adam, moved through a dark passage of sin and suffering, toward a new life beyond time and history. Human history itself was but a page in eternity, one day to be turned and laid aside when all things are made new. The whole pattern was grandly portrayed in *The City of God,* where Augustine speaks, in his opening sentence, of

that most glorious society and celestial city of God's faithful, which is partly seated in the course of these declining times, wherein "he that liveth by faith" is a pilgrim amongst the wicked; and partly in that solid state of eternity, which as yet the other part doth patiently expect, until "righteousness be turned into judgment," being then by the proper excellence to obtain the last victory, and be crowned in perfection of peace.[5]

A cyclical conception of life characterizes almost all mythical thought, in which, as Philip Wheelwright has said, "time spirals rather than marches." [6] We are familiar with one of its expressions in particular, the dying and reborn god whose life cycle merges with that of the changing yet changeless year. Augustine's formulation makes clear the way in which, in the Christian version of the "monomyth," all slighter cycles, of seasons, Great Years, or individual lives, melted into a single gigantic circle comprising the whole of human time. The Creation, the Fall of Man, the Redemption by Christ, and the Last Judgment: these were the key points on the circumference, joined by images of patience and faith, of warfare and victory, of death and life. Thus the Christian view of history repeats, on a grand scale, more primitive life-patterns.

[5] *City of God*, Book I, ch. 1; I, 1.
[6] *The Burning Fountain* (Bloomington, Ind., 1954), p. 164.

In his great central work, Milton embodied definitively and comprehensively the Christian pattern of human destiny. But his total poetic *oeuvre* can also be seen as a set of variations on a single theme, the fruit of the forbidden tree. From the *Nativity*, in which was recorded the death of Pan and the advent of the one true God, to *Samson Agonistes* where fallen man rises phoenix-like from the ashes of his dark fate, Milton traced and retraced the paradigm of loss and return, fall and resurrection. The shadowy journey of life is allegorized in the woodland wanderings of *Comus*, which opens with a "misled and lonely Traveller" benighted in a "leavie Labyrinth." Samson, whose darkness withstands even the blaze of noon, is a "foolish Pilot" shipwrecked in his quest; and even the Christ of *Paradise Regained*, alone in a "pathless Desert," is symbolically an outcast *in exilium vitae temporalis.*

The pattern as a whole can be seen most plainly, before *Paradise Lost*, in *Lycidas*, an accurate and complex transcription of some enduring preoccupations. It is the most rewarding of the shorter poems for the student of myth, and will repay a brief scrutiny as a thematic microcosm of the epic. In it is re-enacted the loss of Paradise that occurs in the life of every individual. The opening lines, with their disturbed note of heavy change and a natural world shattered before fruition, are followed by the description in the third section of this ruined world as it was before death came into it. The pastoral lines on the poets' early lives (23–36) foreshadow in miniature the later image of the Garden where change is merely an elaborate kind of changelessness and time only the quiet alternation of night and day; where the stars rise and set with a motion that is almost like breathing. When we first see Paradise, the sun

Declin'd was hasting now with prone carreer
To th' Ocean Iles, and in th' ascending Scale
Of Heav'n the Starrs that usher Evening rose. (iv.353–55)

Just so, Milton and Edward King inhabit an undisturbed world. They drive their flocks afield in the morning, returning only when

the Star that rose, at Ev'ning, bright,
Toward Heav'ns descent had slop'd his westering wheel. (30–31)

And, as Milton recalls their early-morning labours,

Together both, ere the high Lawns appear'd
Under the opening eye-lids of the morn, (25–26)

so Adam reminds Eve of the task awaiting them:

Tomorrow ere fresh Morning streak the East
With first approach of light, we must be ris'n,
And at our pleasant labour. (iv.623–25)

Such similarities can be accounted for by saying that *Lycidas* and Milton's picture of Eden are products of the same convention; but pastoral was in fact a version of the theme of the Golden Age, which looked back, for Christian poets, to life in Paradise. Pastoral restates symbolically a particular sort of experience that existed actually in the Garden, whether Christian or pagan.

The feeling of harmony in the idyl from *Lycidas* is enhanced by a complex of images that are always positive terms for Milton: temporal cycles, dance, song (poetry), and fecundity (the "fresh dews" of l. 29). The burden of disaster that follows is the heavier because all its elements negate the happy images of "paradise." This scene (37–49) finds an analogue in the events in Eden after the Fall. Milton gives three images for a decay of nature that first occurred in the archetypal Paradise.

> As killing as the Canker to the Rose,
> Or Taint-worm to the weanling Herds that graze,
> Or Frost to Flowers, that their gay wardrop wear,
> When first the White Thorn blows;
> Such, *Lycidas,* thy loss to Shepherds ear. (45–49)

The root of the metaphorical idea is in the unhappy correspondence of nature to man at the Fall, when "pinching cold and scorching heate" first assailed the flowers, and "Beast . . . with Beast gan war."

Loss and decay, fall and death — these mark the first stage of the "universal myth." The second and third stages — the journey of life-in-death and regained Paradise — also appear in Milton's elegy, expressed in a double-stranded water imagery. The "remorseless deep," agent of death, is denied the ordinary life-sustaining power of water in the opening lines when Lycidas is shown weltering "to the *parching* wind"; he is being withered, not revived. On the other hand, streams, rivers, fountains, and springs are the sources of life-giving fresh water. The shepherd's rill, the "wisard stream" of Dee haunted by the Muses, the "gushing brooks" of the vales whose flowers strew King's hearse, are all related to the "other streams" where a reborn Lycidas emerges from darkness into eternal day.

> So *Lycidas* sunk low but mounted high,
> Through the dear might of him that walk'd the waves
> Where other groves, and other streams along,
> With Nectar pure his oozy Lock's he laves. . . . (172–75)

Once more, the lines cast light ahead to the clear paradisal and heavenly streams of *Paradise Lost.*

The emotive structure of *Lycidas* repeats the myth's three-layered plan, moving from a point where only one change — the heavy change of death — is apparent, to the poet's realization that a further transformation will take place and restore the lost, though in an altered form. Through the redemptive power of Christ who walked the waves, taming their destructive power (as, at his birth in the *Nativity*, he "charmed" the raving Ocean), the wheel comes full circle and brings back the peaceful world that was invaded by violence at the beginning. Order and peace, symbolized by the quiet diurnal progress, have returned. While the poet has been singing, the still morn has gone out as it used to do,

> And now the Sun had stretch'd out all the hills,
> And now was dropt into the Western Bay. (190–91)

In *Lycidas,* then, the threefold design of the monomyth is embodied in an intensely personal poem. But the likeness to *Paradise Lost* stops once we have noticed the thematic structure and a few images. *Lycidas* is a condensed, radically metaphorical poem, as its component devices bear witness: an allusive style, interwoven symbols, and the pastoral convention itself, which always has a metaphorical dimension. It is not accidental that the elegy has proved a responsive subject for the interpretive criticism that is most successful when it deals with "oblique" poetry.[7] Milton made an early effort to treat the myth *directly* in the unfinished *Passion,* but failing to discover a satisfactory style and manner for his mythic sub-

[7] During the last decade, a number of articles have been written on the mythological themes in this poem. See: Richard P. Adams, "The Archetypal Pattern of Death and Rebirth in Milton's *Lycidas*," *PMLA,* LXIV (1949), 183–88; J. E. Hardy, "Lycidas," *Kenyon Review,* VII (1945), 99–113; Caroline W. Mayerson, "The Orpheus Image in *Lycidas*," *PMLA,* LXIV (1949), 189–207; Wayne Shumaker, "Flowerets and Sounding Seas: A Study in the Affective Structure of *Lycidas*," *PMLA,* LXVI (1951), 485–94.

ject, and finding it "to be above the yeers he had, when he wrote it," abandoned it. The poem is interesting as an attempt to handle a super-personal theme in the allusive private style. The successful marriage of a mythic subject and a style brilliantly heightened and impersonalized to meet it, was to wait half a lifetime.

THE GOLDEN AGE RESTORED

To understand the structure of *Paradise Lost,* we must have a firm grasp of a mythological content, the Christian paradigm of history, and to this *Lycidas* and the other early poems provide some useful clues. But they cannot supply the other essential knowledge that will help us to comprehend the texture of Milton's epic. For that, we must know something of a mythological form, a mode of experience or "manner of seeing" that is alien both to a logical/abstract articulation of "reality," and to our practical everyday experience.

Paradise Lost is not oblique, but a direct rendering of certain stupendous realities now known only indirectly in the symbolic signatures of earthly life. Theology and popular opinion for generations had accustomed Christians to imagining life in Eden as unlike everyday life in certain distinct ways; human knowledge, and its objects as well, differed there from ordinary modes of seeing and being. The poet whose subject was Paradise set out, therefore, to reproduce forms of experience that no longer existed, and their peculiar conditions imposed upon his endeavors stylistic and technical limits. So, in his prayer for illumination in Book III, Milton asks for the vision that will enable him to reproduce a world hitherto inaccessible to poetry, that will reach beyond the mists of history and the confusions of a fallen world, to look on something else:

> So much the rather thou Celestial light
> Shine inward, and the mind through all her powers
> Irradiate, there plant eyes, all mist from thence
> Purge and disperse, that I may see and tell
> Of things invisible to mortal sight. (iii.51–55)

Sir Herbert Grierson has numbered Milton among "prophetic" poets; and Taine, oracular as usual, refers to him as "héritier des voyants hébreux, dernier des voyants scandinaves." [8]

But what is the object, in poetry, of this sort of second sight? Blake, whose own vision matched Milton's in apocalyptic power, suggested it, writing of himself: "The Nature of my Work is Visionary or Imaginative; it is an Endeavour to Restore what the Ancients call'd the Golden Age." [9] The cyclical pattern of myth, in particular the great cycle of history, combined with the notion that at the end something once lost is regained, tends to divide the mythic world-landscape into two parts: on one hand, the mutable, fleeting, time-subdued stream of racial and individual history; on the other, "the solid state of eternity," including both the lost and the regained. Between the State of Innocence and the Golden Age Restored stretches the wilderness of the world, a temporal span separating, for the time being, two eternities. This configuration is traced at the end of *Paradise Lost* by the archangel Michael. Standing still within a timeless world about to become the past, Adam foresees a timeless future.

[8] Hippolyte Taine, *Histoire de la littérature anglaise* (5 vols., Paris, 1866–69), I, 56.
[9] *A Vision of the Last Judgment, Poetry and Prose of William Blake,* ed. Geoffrey Keynes (Bloomsbury [London], 1932), p. 830.

How soon hath thy prediction, Seer blest,
Measur'd this transient World, the Race of time,
Till time stand fixt: beyond is all abyss,
Eternitie, whose end no eye can reach. (xii.553–56)

Information about the two eternities inevitably merged, so that prophecy was an element in the mythic recreations of the past. Milton, like most of his contemporaries, used Revelation as evidence for the War in Heaven; [10] as Denis Saurat observes, "It is a sort of law in prophetic imagination that the end should be like the beginning, and these texts became . . . a precious source of knowledge about the origins." [11]

The distinction between historical experience within time, and the mythic experience beyond time in the remote past or future, which he was to embody in *Paradise Lost*, was familiar to Milton from contemporary descriptions which helped to define the "manner of seeing" that was necessary if he were to represent the world of unfallen man; it may also be negatively helpful in suggesting some poetic devices that could *not* be used. Christian epistemology recognized two kinds of knowledge, appropriate to the dissimilar experiences of mythic and historical man. Our earthly experience, as the figure of the pilgrimage suggests, is difficult, intricate, and time-consuming. The exhausting journey of Dante is an intensified version of the trials we must all endure, the mountain of Purgatory an ancient symbol for the progress toward lost innocence. The lady of Milton's Sonnet IX seeks to join those who "labour up the hill of Heav'nly Truth"; and

10 See, *e.g., Christian Doctrine,* Book I, ch. ix: "Michael, the leader of the angels, is introduced in the capacity of a hostile commander waging war with the prince of the devils, the armies on both sides being drawn out in battle array, and separating after a doubtful conflict. Rev. 12:7–8." *SM,* 985. Quotations from Milton's prose, unless otherwise indicated, are also from *The Student's Milton,* abbreviated hereafter as *SM.*

11 *Milton, Man and Thinker,* 2nd ed. (London, 1944), p. 216.

the image of the mountain with the light of eternal verity at its crest and the abyss at its root later provided the geography of *Paradise Lost* itself, where the narrative moves from the depth of darkness and ignorance to the "fountain of light" in Heaven.[12]

The Fall of Man is, therefore, to be understood not only as a lapse into sin, but as a retreat from truth; the search for "heavenly Truth" and for lost Paradise thus become subjective and objective aspects of a single pilgrimage. The cause of our perplexities is exposed by Milton in a celebrated paragraph of his prose, where knowledge is represented as the power of penetrating chaos to restore order.

Good and evil we know in the field of this world grow up together almost inseparably; and the knowledge of good is so involved and interwoven with the knowledge of evil, and in so many cunning resemblances hardly to be discerned, that those confused seeds which were imposed upon Psyche as an incessant labour to cull out, and sort asunder, were not more intermixed. It was from out the rind of one apple tasted, that the knowledge of good and evil, as two twins cleaving together, leaped forth into the world. And perhaps this is that doom which Adam fell into of knowing good and evil; that is to say, of knowing good by evil. As therefore the state of man now is; what wisdom can there be to choose, what continence to forbear, without the knowledge of evil? [13]

[12] Compare Petrarch's allegorical moralizing on his ascent of Mont Ventoux: "On the highest summit is set the end of all, the goal toward which our pilgrimage is directed. Every man wants to arrive there." Ficino, a Platonist exiled from his true home, lamented (in *Five Questions Concerning the Mind*): "We seek the highest summits of Mount Olympus. We inhabit the abyss of the lowest valley." *The Renaissance Philosophy of Man*, ed. Ernst Cassirer, Paul Oskar Kristeller, and John Herman Randall (Chicago, 1948), pp. 40, 209.

Bacon made the same allegorical equation as Milton in his essay on Truth: "a hill not to be commanded, and where the air is always clear and serene." *Essays*, Everyman's Library (London, 1943), p. 4.

[13] *Areopagitica, SM*, p. 738.

When our first parents ate the apple, good and evil leaped forth as a monstrous birth, compounding elements that had hitherto been separate. This corruption, this muddying of the pure waters of truth, was the object of Satan's voyage: "Earth with Hell To mingle and involve" (ii.383–84). The theme of the obscure quest for knowledge through the wood of the world, the "incessant labour" of understanding, is thus explained, and in a sense justified, by the original myth of the parting of warring atoms, and the return to Chaos by Satan's agency at the Fall.

Unlike the twins who represented good and evil in old versions of the cosmic war, these are Siamese twins, "cleaving together." Simple dualism is succeeded by duplicity: a world where good is known by evil, and evil may wear the disguises of good, as it does when Satan, "artificer of fraud," puts on the likeness of a cherub in Book III of *Paradise Lost*. The deceitfulness of things makes life a struggle, a hill to be labored up, a maze of pitfalls, a mass of confusions to be "culled out and sorted asunder." Whitehead has defined truth as "the conformation of Appearance to Reality"; after Satan's rebellion and man's sin, the two are no longer congruent.

The daily warfare of the wayfaring Christian is, therefore, not only a contest between good and evil, but an effort to see them clearly. The goal of the life journey can be called regained paradise; just as accurately, it can be seen as the state of man *in* paradise: possessing the capacity to perceive truth, not by following the roundabout paths we now take, but directly. This is achieved by our regeneration in Christ; then, Milton wrote, "is the understanding restored in great part to its primitive clearness." [14] Education, too, may assist the

[14] *Christian Doctrine*, II, xxi. *SM*, pp. 1016–17.

process: "The end then of learning is to repair the ruins of our first parents by regaining to know God aright." [15] Milton, like his "sage and serious" master, Spenser, was troubled by the discord between the unmistakable light of truth and the intricate ways leading to it — "the perpetual stumble of conjecture and disturbance in this our dark voyage." [16]

Counterbalancing these gloomy and strenuous views of human knowledge were the descriptions of understanding as it had been in the infancy of the individual or the race, and would be again in the life after death or after the end of the world, when "primitive clearness" had been restored. A stanza of DuBartas' *Divine Weekes* draws a pointed comparison between "after" and "before":

> But our now-*knowledge* hath, for tedious train,
> A drooping life, and over-racked brain,
> A face forlorn, a sad and sullen fashion,
> A restlesse toyl, and Care's self-pining passion.
> Knowledge was then even the soule's soul for light,
> The spirit's calm Port, and Lanthorn shining bright
> To strait-stept feet: cleer knowledg; not confus'd:
> Not sowr, but sweet: not gotten, but infus'd.[17]

A paragraph by Traherne on his childhood, emphasizing the same "infus'd" or intuitive knowledge that avoided the "tedious train" of discursive reason, links two states of innocence:

Adam in Paradise had not more sweet and curious apprehensions of the world, than I when I was a child. My knowledge was Divine. I knew by intuition those things which since my Apostasy, I collected again by the highest reason. My very ignorance

15 *Of Education, SM,* p. 726.
16 *Reason of Church Government, SM,* p. 506.
17 Second Week, First Day, Part I, *Works of Joshua Sylvester,* I, 102.

was advantageous. I seemed as one brought into the Estate of Innocence.[18]

Spenser, too, read into a happier past a Wordsworthian innocency of vision.

> Antique age, yet in the infancie
> Of time, did live then like an innocent,
> In simple truth and blameless chastitie,
> Ne then of guile had made experiment. (*F.Q.* IV.viii.30)

The condition of the blessed dead restores the simplicity lost by Adam and every child. Donne, whose pilgrim toiled up the mountain of truth, also traced the progress of the soul to Paradise, where he promised that it should "see all things despoyl'd of fallacies": "in heaven thou straight know'st all." [19] This vision is developed in a sermon, and explicitly contrasted with our ways of knowing on earth.

Our curiosity shall have this noble satisfaction, we shall know how the Angels know, by knowing as they know. We shall not pass from Author to Author, as in a Grammar School, nor from Art to Art, as in an University; but . . . God shall create us all Doctors in a minute. That great Library, those infinite Volumes of the Books of Creatures, shall be taken away, quite away, no more Nature; . . . no more preaching, no more reading of Scriptures, and that great School-Mistress, Experience, and Observation shall be remov'd, no new thing to be done, and in an instant, I shall know more, then they all could reveal unto me.[20]

Similarly, Castiglione's Bembo rehearses the joys awaiting the neo-Platonic adept whose soul, rapt to Heaven, "hath no

[18] Thomas Traherne, *Centuries of Meditations*, ed. B. Dobell (London, 1908), p. 151.
[19] *The Second Anniversary*, ll. 295–99.
[20] *The Works of John Donne, D.D.*, ed. Henry Alford (6 vols., London, 1839), VI, 184–85.

more neede of the discourse of reason, for being chaunged
into an Angell, she understandeth all thinges that may be
understood." [21]

The common elements in these accounts need hardly be
insisted upon. All record a kind of experience direct, intuitive, outgoing "discourse of reason," independent of previous
experience, instantaneous, and "simple." They may be
summed up in the words of St. Paul, whose greatest rhetoric
balanced between the realities of time and eternity. "For
now we see through a glass, darkly" — the glass of time and
space, and our fallen condition; "but then face to face" —
then, long ago or someday.

In celestial paradise the crooked images will be reassembled or "collected" so that we can see again the one truth
face to face; and a similar condition was generally thought to
have prevailed in terrestrial paradise before the Fall. Sir John
Davies' account of Adam and Eve as wise ancients includes
familiar details:

> Their skill infusde did passe all arts
> That euer were, before, or since the Flood;
>
> . . . their reason's eye was sharpe and cleare,
> And (as an eagle can behold the sunne)
> Could haue approacht th' Eternall Light as neere
> As the intellectuall angels could haue done.[22]

Aquinas had given a more technical account of Adam's "angelic" understanding, which passed through objects to their
"intelligible effects" — that is, concepts — immediately.[23]

21 *The Book of the Courtier,* trans. Sir Thomas Hoby, Everyman's Library
(London, 1948), p. 319.
22 *The Works in Verse and Prose,* ed. Alexander B. Grosart (3 vols., London, 1869–76), I, 43–44.
23 *Summa Theologica,* I. 94.4, *Basic Writings,* ed. Anton C. Pegis (2 vols.,
New York, 1945), I, 903–904.

Milton was following this tradition when he declared, "Certainly without extraordinary wisdom [Adam] could not have given names to the whole animal creation with such sudden intelligence." [24] What most impressed him about this perfect discernment was its speed and immediacy; he repeats the point in *Paradise Lost* as Adam speaks of himself when he first saw the beasts.

> I nam'd them, as they pass'd, and understood
> Thir Nature, with such knowledg God endu'd
> My sudden apprehension. (viii.352–54)

The stylistic consequences of an effort to restore this innocency of vision in poetry may now be more clearly observed. Poetic language, axiomatically, is figurative language; and yet, to recall Bernard Shaw's phrase, "Heaven cannot be described by metaphor." As the source rather than the product of history and nature, the myth is not to be illuminated by analogies with historical events and natural objects. A mythic event does not stand for anything else; it is what everything else stands for, "most simply, onely like it selfe, and partner of non other." [25] Metaphorical or (broadly speaking) allegorical styles in which meaning is enacted or adumbrated by analogous incidents and symbols, are therefore inappropriate for a poem that finds its subject in myth. Blake's account of "visionary" poetry is again relevant:

24 *Christian Doctrine*, I, vii. *SM*, p. 981. See also the remark in *Tetrachordon:* "Adam, who had the wisdom given him to know all creatures, and to name them according to their properties, no doubt but had the gift to discern perfectly . . ." *SM*, p. 659. This stress on the naming of the beasts, evidence of man's "sovereignty and power" based on his superior perception and knowledge, was a commonplace; cf. Bacon: "Whensoever he shall be able to call the creatures by their true names he shall again command them." *Of the Interpretation of Nature, Works*, III, 222.

25 The phrase appears in Pietro Bembo's eulogy of the Idea of Beauty. Castiglione, *Courtier*, p. 320.

Fable or Allegory are a totally distinct & inferior kind of Poetry. Vision or Imagination is a Representation of what Eternally Exists, Really & Unchangeably. Fable or Allegory is Form'd by the daughters of Memory. . . . The Hebrew Bible & the Gospel of Jesus are not Allegory, but Eternal Vision or Imagination of All that Exists. . . . Allegory & Vision ought to be known as Two Distinct Things.[26]

Myth is inaccessible to metaphor/allegory not only because it is itself the "cause" of metaphor, but also because the "objects" that inhabit the landscape of myth are unlike those distinguished by our habitual ways of thinking, which may be loosely called logical or analytical. They are both concrete and universal rather than concrete *or* universal, creatures permeated with "meanings" that in later ages became conceptualized and abstracted. Failure to recognize the distinction between unified "mythic" seeing and our own atomized knowledge, leads to the sort of one-sided interpretation of myth that was examined in Chapter I. Ernst Cassirer observes that such commentators look on myth "as an allegorical, symbolic language concealing a secret meaning, a purely ideal content which can be glimpsed behind its images." In fact, however, the images are the reality.

If we examine myth itself, . . . we see that this separation of the ideal from the real, this distinction between a world of immediate reality and a world of mediate signification, this opposition of "image" and "object," is alien to it. Only observers who no longer live in it but reflect on it read such distinctions into myth.[27]

26 *Vision of Last Judgment, Poetry and Prose*, pp. 828–29.

27 *Mythical Thought*, p. 38. Owen Barfield, in an influential book on the origins of language, has spoken in similar terms of the "primitive" mode of seeing and experiencing. "You may imply, if you choose, . . . that the earliest words in use were 'the names of sensible, material objects' *and nothing more* — only, in that case, you must suppose the 'sensible objects'

In *Paradise Lost,* Milton represented the unified, immediate images of the earliest created beings; one sign that he recognized, however implicitly, the technical demands attaching to this aim, is his abandonment of allegory, the poetic method that most obviously insists on the separation in thought of idea from image, before he came to write his poem. The plans for tragedies on a similar theme all include allegorical personages; Heavenly Love, Ignorance, Labour, Mercy, Wisdom, Faith, move through the sketches in the Cambridge Manuscript, only to disappear at some point before the epic took final shape. The outline for "Adam unparadiz'd" shows fallen man among reproachful abstractions: "Conscience in a shape accuses him. Justice cites him to the place whither Jehova call'd for him." [28] We cannot know Milton's reasons for dismissing these plans; but we can say that they would have been quite out of key with the mythical vision that was finally embodied in *Paradise Lost.*

Milton's celebrated description of poetry as "simple, sensuous and passionate" was made to distinguish it from logic and rhetoric, the discursive forms of expression; the phrase may be supposed to indicate an intuitive, concrete expressiveness where "passion" and meaning are implicit in the images. Poetry is "simple" in the sense not of "uncomplex," but of "single," as Miss Wallerstein has pointed out in her discussion of Milton's essay; this quality is "a single, living, and unified essence which in poetry immediately reflects Nature and the divine essence behind Nature; not divided and ana-

---

themselves to have been something more. . . . Afterwards, in the development of language and thought, these single meanings split up into contrasted pairs — the abstract and the concrete, particular and general, objective and subjective." *Poetic Diction* (London, 1928), pp. 70–71.

[28] Cambridge MS., *SM,* pp. 1128–33. Milton did, of course, retain two allegorical figures in *Paradise Lost* — Sin and Death — for reasons that will appear later.

lyzed as discursive reason divides." [29] The mythic image or personage is more comprehensive, "simple," and unified than any concept derived from it by analytic thought. Though Milton's words apply to poetry in general, they are fulfilled with special force in *Paradise Lost*, where the objects of the prehistoric world are still clear and distinct, not yet sunk into the ambiguity that perplexes our fallen perceptions. A pertinent expansion of Milton's remarks, and a description of his practice, can be found in some further sentences by Cassirer.

As [logic] tends toward expansion, implication, and systematic connection, [myth] tends toward concentration, telescoping, separate characterization. . . . In mythic conception . . . things are not taken for what they mean indirectly, but for their immediate appearance; they are taken as pure presentations, and embodied in the imagination. . . . In the myth nothing has any significance or being save what is given in tangible reality. Here is no "reference" or "meaning"; every content of consciousness to which the mind is directed is immediately translated into terms of actual presence and effectiveness.[30]

The qualities here indicated — concreteness, self-completeness, immediacy, uniqueness, clear-cut but complex appearances, the dynamic activity called "effectiveness" — characterize the *dramatis personae* of *Paradise Lost*.

When we speak, then, of myth, we must speak not only of a story, the images and events of primordial reality that have determined our history; but also of the patterns, in narrative and verse-texture, that naturally express those images and that reality. As important to *Paradise Lost* as the fable itself

[29] Ruth Wallerstein, *Studies in Seventeenth Century Poetic* (University of Wisconsin [Madison], 1950), p. 32.
[30] *Language and Myth*, trans. Susanne K. Langer (New York, 1946), pp. 56–57.

are the myth's circular, returning shape, and its innocence
of vision harking back to an experience older than any individual life. Milton made his poem from these elements,
though he knew nothing of myth in the technical sense, and
the jargon of professional mythographers would have been
barbarous dissonance to his ear. His poem was an English
epic, his manner the grand style practiced by his peers, classical and contemporary. Yet the name we give to his realities
is unimportant. Their nature, and his goal, are suggested in
a phrase of Susanne Langer: "virtual memory." Mrs. Langer
speaks of "the virtual character of so-called 'aesthetic
objects,'" the illusion, or symbol of experience, produced in
every work of art. Art can never conjure tangible reality into
literal existence — it is not magic; but it can give us a faithful equivalent in the form of a "virtual" reality. The painter
works not in actual but in virtual space; the poet creates "virtual memory, or history in the mode of an experienced
Past." [31] The special history of *Paradise Lost* is prehistory;
the memory evoked is something like racial memory, if we
can use the term without philosophical commitment. The
illusion of Milton's epic is "virtual myth": in it, we come as
close as we ever can to the experience of living in the lost
garden. *Paradise Lost* does not represent Milton's, or anyone else's, ordinary manner of thinking about the truths of
Christianity; for that, we may look *inter alia* to the *Christian
Doctrine*. What the poem does is to allow us, temporarily, to
share a manner of seeing that will capture accurately the
outlines of a peculiar kind of reality; and to make it do this
Milton, guided by the natural movement of the myth itself,
invented a series of techniques profoundly original, and
strange with the strangeness of the long-forgotten — among
them a style reverberatory and unmetaphorical, and a "spa-

31 *Feeling and Form* (New York, 1953), pp. 48, 279.

tial" structural pattern of interlocking, mutually dependent parts.

The first fifty lines of the poem state, in conventional and condensed form, Milton's subject and purpose; they frame the illusory virtual world that we are shortly to enter. With a deliberate modulation of tenses, Milton draws us into it, and we see Satan face to face:

> But his doom
> Reserv'd him to more wrath, for now the thought
> Both of lost happiness and lasting pain
> Torments him; round he throws his baleful eyes . . . (i.53–56)

From lookers-on, we have become active rememberers of a forgotten universe. Milton in his youthful fancy had made visible the archetypal Platonic man —

> Sive in remota forte terrarum plaga
> Incedit ingens hominis archetypus gigas,
> Et diis tremendus erigit celsum caput
> Atlante major portitore syderum.[32]

In *Paradise Lost,* the "original" and mythic ancestor of humanity is released from the remote regions of the earth and restored to his rightful place in a remote region of time, "aeternus, incorruptus, aequaevus polo, Unusque et universus," larger than life-size, simpler and clearer than the figures of our world, but crucial for our proper understanding of it.

[32] "Or perchance in some far-distant part of the world he moves, a giant huge, this Archetype of Man, and lifts his lofty head, affrighting the gods, taller than Atlas who bears the burden of the stars." *De idea Platonica* . . . ll. 21–24. Translated by N. G. McCrea.

CHAPTER

III

STRUCTURAL PATTERNS IN
PARADISE LOST

THE MAGIC MOUNTAIN

Writing of "the plan of *Paradise Lost,*" Johnson complained: "But these truths are too important to be new. . . . Being therefore not new, they raise no unaccustomed emotion in the mind; what we knew before, we cannot learn; what is not unexpected, cannot surprise." [1] The author of the poem may be supposed to have recognized this limitation of his subject — if it is a limitation; his recognition is in fact contained in the Argument to Book I and in the first fifty lines, which summarize the "story," thus acknowledging that "surprise" is not to be factitiously striven for. Indeed, it is precisely *accustomed* emotion to which Milton makes his appeal. Our interest in a myth depends largely upon foreknowledge; its familiar story is something we have always with us, to which our attention returns periodically for recognition and affirmation.

The poet whose subject is myth strives to promote, therefore, not learning but knowledge; to evoke not surprise but

[1] *Lives of the Poets,* I, 182.

44

acknowledgment; to produce not development but revelation, not an introduction to something new, but a deepened understanding of something old. Consequently, the "normal" straightforward narrative patterns traditional to story-tellers will be inappropriate; suspense will be replaced by the tacit comment of interconnecting temporal threads. The mythical narrative slights chronology in favor of a folded structure which continually returns upon itself, or a spiral that circles about a single center; in this, it reproduces the very shape of the myth itself, which is circularly designed for resonance and cross-reference. The poem will be built from a blueprint rather than a map; because suspense is neglected and expanding implications are stressed, it will have the third dimension of depth, whereas the ordinary story is built in the two surface dimensions and the fourth, time. Telling of the story *qua* story is minimized by the mythologist; and, as Hardy said of his historical myth in *The Dynasts,* "foreknowledge is assumed to fill in the curves."[2]

These characteristics are visible, of course, in the *Iliad* and the *Aeneid,* acknowledged by Milton as "diffuse models" of the epic form. Homer, his imagination "at the same time stimulated and limited" by his listeners' foreknowledge of the tale of Troy, could not invent major new episodes;[3] on the other hand, the story's very familiarity freed him in another direction, enabling the audience to follow without confusion his reordering of the old material. Homer need not explain that Troy is to fall; tacit anticipation of its fall makes possible [proleptic] ironies like that in Agamemnon's speech in Book IX:

Come then, do as I say, let us all be won over; let us

2 Thomas Hardy, Preface to *The Dynasts* (3 vols., New York, 1904), I, ix.
3 Richmond Lattimore, Introduction to his translation of *The Iliad of Homer* (Chicago, 1951), p. 21.

> run away with our ships to the beloved land of our fathers
> since no longer now shall we capture Troy of the wide ways.[4]

An inverted analogue to these effects can be found in The Book of Job, which Milton singled out as "a brief model" of the epic.[5] Job exhibits a number of mythic motifs, such as the spirit's challenge and the three tempters; and also, more pertinently, an iterative structure that was to provide a plan for *Paradise Regained* and *Samson Agonistes.* This brief epic, treating "of deeds Above Heroic, though in secret done" (*P.R.,* i.14–15), owes its effect to our familiarity with a pattern which is created only to be thunderously broken when God at last speaks out of the whirlwind. This time the *design,* not, as in Homer, the *matter* of the story, provides the recognizable element. The fall from good to evil fortune, the reiteration of insoluble problems, the climactic solution by a divine agent, the return to the opening situation on a new level: this narrative pattern, cumulative and retrospective rather than simply chronological, evokes in us the kind of attention that we give to a recognized rather than a novel story. Thus the "foreknowledge" common to mythic literature is here attached to the shape of the tale and its legendary motifs; in the *Iliad* and *Paradise Lost,* to the fable itself. Job, and Milton's adaptations of its form in his last poems, are didactic works which dramatize the internal landscapes of psychology and morals rather than the external mythic realities of *Paradise Lost;* their "originality" is, therefore, located in the qualities of those psychic landscapes, while in the great epic it is the shape, the handling, that is "original."

F. W. Bateson has described poetry as engaged in "a continual struggle to abrogate time"; [6] all the works discussed

---

4 *The Iliad,* trans. R. Lattimore, ix.26–28.
5 *Reason of Church Government, SM,* p. 525.
6 *English Poetry and the English Language* (Oxford, 1934), p. 18.

external mythic realities of PL.

[ ]: abolish

above achieve the abrogation of time on a massive scale. In *Paradise Lost,* Milton shows a supreme inventiveness in using devices of emphasis that will serve to make his reader aware of recurrences. To understate the effect of time, he must employ, nevertheless, the techniques of a temporal art; it is an illusion, only, of timelessness that is achieved, for time is consumed even as we read. But early critics who discussed the epic recognized a distinction between its approach to chronology and that of the historical or narrative modes. Johnson, praising "the writer of an epick poem," pressed on him the need to view his subject as a whole.

History must supply the writer with the rudiments of narration, which he must improve and exalt by a nobler art, must animate by dramatick energy, and diversify by retrospection and anticipation.[7]

"Retrospection and anticipation" are the keys to both epic and mythological patterns.

We have already seen that in mythical thought, time is typically felt as a returning, cyclical pattern, rather than as an infinitely prolonged line, moving relentlessly from a lost past to a changed future. In Eden, "Sin, not Time, first wraught the change" (ix.70); time is the medium of a uniform experience, not yet of change. This attitude can be found embodied in *Paradise Lost* in two major ways: in the picture of the Garden, especially as it is reflected in the intuitions of unfallen man; and in the organization and structure of the poem as a whole. "Structure" is a protean term, particularly as applied to Milton's epic, where almost every detail can be architecturally justified. In this chapter, I shall discuss chiefly the management and placing of incidents to form an ordered pattern that is strikingly un-chronological; subsequent chap-

---

[7] *Lives of the Poets,* I, 170.

ters will show how other elements in the poem, particularly the imagery and the major "sub-plot," the career of Satan, reinforce this basic framework.

It may be said that the structure of *Paradise Lost* is explained by the fact that Milton was writing an epic and was therefore constrained by well-defined rules of narrative. But this claim, however true, is of limited relevance. *Paradise Lost* is not a typical epic, if by typical one means written in conformity with the precepts set out by Renaissance theory. Most of the early critics of Milton complained that the poem violates these canons in one way or another, and the poet himself had early left it an open question "whether the rules of Aristotle are herein strictly to be kept, or nature to be followed, which in them that know art, and use judgment, is no transgression, but an enriching of art." [8] In fact, each of the great classical epics follows a "nature" of its own, enriching art with a design to suit the subject, and nothing can be proved by arguments from precedent. As Milton's intention and subject matter diverged from those of Homer, Virgil, or Tasso, "the rules of Aristotle" were left further behind. In the opinion of Coleridge, *Paradise Lost* not only emulates but improves upon precedent. He wrote that the *Iliad* and its peers are "but single chapters from the volume of history," whereas Milton's epic has "the totality of the poem as distinguished from the *ab ovo* birth and parentage, or straight line, of history." [9] *Paradise Lost* ranges further in time and space than Homer's and Virgil's epics, yet it produces also an effect of greater concentration and sustained intensity — the result, I think, of the clearly-defined architectural "stage" on which the myth is enacted.

8 *Reason of Church Government, SM,* p. 525.
9 *Coleridge's Miscellaneous Criticism,* ed. Thomas Middleton Raysor (Cambridge, Mass., 1936), p. 161.

Milton borrowed such epic devices as accorded with his purpose, and discarded those that did not. He did, of course, find useful principles for the reconstruction of the myth in a gradually evolved epic genre that had been the vehicle of mythical material many times before. The *Iliad*, we are told, is composed of elements from "folk tale, fiction, and saga"; [10] the *Odyssey* proved amenable to allegorical and mythic readings by medieval commentators; in *Beowulf* the waste land theme is reincarnated; and the *Aeneid* may be read as a national myth, explaining the origins of a culture in the historical but miraculous founding of a city —

> Genus unde Latinum,
> Albanique patres, atque altae moenia Romae. (i.6–7) [11]

It has been suggested, too, that Milton's initial statement of his subjects — disobedience, woe, restoration — corresponds to the pattern of Virgil's — the fall of Troy, the journey, the founding of Rome.[12] The mission of Aeneas is to found a second Troy and so bring his men and household gods home again; it re-embodies the theme of loss and return.

Virgil's epic concentrates on return and the temporal motif of the journey, Milton's on loss and the reconstruction of what was lost. The ruined paradise is, most obviously, the Garden, which gives the poem its spatial and structural focus; but in a wider sense, there were lost also those visions of a world-order imparted by the angel in Books V and VIII. Milton set out to rebuild this whole Creation in *Paradise Lost,*

10 See Rhys Carpenter, *Folk Tale, Fiction and Saga in the Homeric Epics* (Berkeley and Los Angeles, 1946).

11 "Whence came the Latin race, the lords of Alba, and the walls of lofty Rome." Translated by H. Rushton Fairclough. *Virgil,* Loeb Classical Library (2 vols., Cambridge, Mass., 1953), I, 240–41.

12 Arthur Barker, "Structural Pattern in *Paradise Lost,*" *PQ,* XXVIII (1949), 17–18.

and his comprehensive design led, presumably, to the early abandonment of the dramatic forms projected in the Cambridge Manuscript. His theme, viewed *sub specie aeternitatis* as he more and more came to see it, made a completed, not an incomplete pattern; was no longer a tragedy but a divine comedy, and so demanded the promise of a *Paradiso* at the end as well as the beginning of the story. Formally, too, the theme had clearly burst the bounds of drama. The fate of Dryden when he set out to dramatize Milton's poem is instructive. Most of the elements that make it truly mythical depend on its modified epic structure, and so were necessarily abandoned in Dryden's operatic version. *The State of Innocence* is focused on Adam and Eve in the Garden; so is *Paradise Lost;* but when Milton's gigantic three-tiered stage is left behind, the crucial importance of their doings evaporates.

For a dramatic scheme unfolding itself in time, Milton substituted a design offered by epic tradition but shaped to his own ends. It is a plan that can be called architectural in the strict sense. *Paradise Lost* is meant to be seen, is only rightly seen, as a great *structure* — somewhat as Satan comes upon the new universe, the divine work of art, at the end of his quest, and

> Looks down with wonder at the sudden view
> Of all this World at once. (iii.542–43)

The simile immediately following compares his vision to a scout's view of a city, complex but single and glorious, "with glistering Spires and Pinnacles adornd" (550). It is an image that exactly conveys the effect produced by the poem itself, a solid and intricate thing that can be seen as a whole. Milton's celebrated architectonic power found its supreme challenge in *Paradise Lost*, where his problem was to embody physical or spatial intuitions in a temporal medium. To say that the plan of the poem is spatial is not to say that a sense of time is never present in it, or that it is static. The background, indeed, stands still, but against it the most violent and the most delicate action and movement take place; in the distance, leading away from or back to it, are the radiations of historic time. Milton's historical sense, like St. Augustine's, combined a mythic awareness of the timeless City of God with a vision of the flux of centuries eddying round it in withdrawal and return. In the poem, time incessantly speaks the same words, much as it turned from day to night and to day again in the peaceful world of Eden. *Paradise Lost* is a poem of intension rather than extension, its shape a cone where meanings are deepened or heightened, but their direction and configuration not essentially changed. Although, as A. S. P. Woodhouse has said, the poem "moves toward an end," [13] it is an end in the teleological sense, a final cause which has been foreseen since the beginning.

A poetic design cannot enter our consciousness directly, as physical space can. But the geography of *Paradise Lost* provides a medium in which motion can take place without the awareness of temporal process — duration — that usually accompanies it; the design is dynamic as architecture is, the eye being carried through various movements against an underlying stability.

The profoundest sensation which we derive from space is not so much that of extension as of permanence. . . . When movement is apprehended through the eye it takes place, so to speak, within the static framework, and the psychological impact of the framework is much more powerful than that of the vibrations which occur within its limits. [14]

13 "Pattern in *Paradise Lost*," *UTQ*, XXII (1952–53), 117.
14 Roger Sessions, "The Composer and his Message," *The Intent of the Artist*, ed. Augusto Centeno (Princeton, 1950), p. 106.

Milton has created this sense of permanence, of "movement apprehended through the eye . . . within the static framework," in *Paradise Lost*. The vibrations of history, created by the myth, are limited by and subordinate to a frame that is different in kind, immune to change.

The awareness of time as merely a function of a larger divine plan was manifested, in one way or another, in most literary versions of the Christian myth. It produced such effects as "anachronism" in the medieval mysteries, which asserted the perpetual re-enactment of key episodes and discounted "historical" change; or again, the powerful system of mutually-reflecting mirrors that composes the *Divine Comedy*. The same sensation, of events moving in an extratemporal scale, can be perceived in the earlier parts of the Old Testament where myth rather than chronicle provides the raw material. Erich Auerbach has noted how, in the Abraham and Isaac story, time is suspended like "a holding of the breath," and temporal indications serve another purpose than the unfolding of a "plot." "So 'early in the morning' is given, not as an indication of time, but for the sake of its ethical significance; it is intended to express the resolution, the promptness, the punctual obedience of the sorely tried Abraham." And as we might expect, the *place* of the sacrifice is important not as naturalistic geography, but as epiphany; it shows forth the intentions of God, immanent even in the landscape. "Jeruel is significant not so much as the goal of an earthly journey, . . . as through its special election, through its relation to God, who designated it as the scene of the act." [15]

Milton, of course, was a student of the past and did not underestimate the pressures of time. But time in the poem, as in other mythic writings, is indefinite, not sharply

[15] *Mimesis: The Representation of Reality in Western Literature*, trans. Willard R. Trask (Princeton, 1953), p. 10.

measured, and often almost suspended, while *areas* are charged with meaning. As one critic has happily said, "The configuration of Milton's Heaven, Hell, Chaos, Limbo, planetary spheres and earth is a map of spiritual forces as well as of physical areas." [16] Milton lived in the age of Descartes' spatial physics and Spinoza's geometric metaphysics; spatial imagining was part of his mental climate. The long view of time as illusory, telescoped into a single vision, had been often adopted in fancy by Christian writers, particularly the adepts in paradox: Sir Thomas Browne could claim that though his grave was England, his dying place was Paradise.[17] This ability to apprehend time as a completed pattern gives it immediately a spatial quality; past and future become not periods, but places. Writing of Heaven and the little heaven of Paradise, Milton by a powerful releasing act of the imagination transposed the intuitive single glance of God into the poem's mythical structure. Our vision of history becomes, for the time being, that of the Creator "whose eye Views all things at one view" (ii. 189–90); like him, we are stationed on a "prospect high Wherein past, present, future he beholds" (iii.77–78). As Charles Singleton has written of the *Divine Comedy*:

This is a vision not of things as we should wish them to be but of things as they are. These are things which even before they

[16] M. M. Mahood, *Poetry and Humanism* (New Haven, 1950), p. 177.

[17] The seventeenth century's preoccupation with the ideal of intuitive knowledge that transcends man's bondage to "discursive reason" has been classed as the "heresy of angelism" by Jacques Maritain. It is important to remember that on this point Milton himself was orthodox. Even in the unfallen world of *Paradise Lost,* where the full effect of time has not yet overtaken mankind, Adam is warned that *human* knowledge is limited: "discourse Is oftest yours, the latter [intuition] most is ours," the angel insists (v.488–89). Milton, in writing the poem, was not wholly obedient to the command to "be lowly wise," any more than Pope presumed not God to scan in the *Essay on Man.* Yet we may take his prayer to the Heavenly Muse as sober and reverent; the poet was gifted with second sight, a more than human sight, that he might exemplify "what religious, what glorious and magnificent use might be made of poetry, both in divine and human things." *Of Education, SM,* p. 729.

are seen are submitted to the lap of God; and because of this, when they are seen they are objective. They do not stand in illusory space. *They stand in the space that God stands in.*[18]

The means of translating the story from time into "God's space" are various. They include accumulation of meaning in words that shoot invisible virtue through the poem, parallel actions, epic similes of a heightened relevance, and a symmetrical architectonic structure. Most important of all is the creation of definite physical areas whose relation to each other and to the actors conveys an implicit "moral" meaning.

The epic practice of beginning *in medias res* was a primary tool; this convention allowed Milton to substitute for the *ab ovo* birth of the story a plan that was spatially coherent, rising from the deepest part of his universe to Heaven, and falling back again. It prepared the way, also, for a poem based on recurrent cycles and the reverberation of key images. In *Paradise Lost,* the midst of things, chronologically, is precisely *not* the mid-point of space; it is the bottom of Hell, the lowest point of physical reality, where the foundations of the pattern can most meaningfully be laid. Since the poem is to be spatially oriented, the spatial mid-point must occupy the center; so chronological displacement is necessary, and is permitted, even required, by epic convention. Milton makes all this clear in his opening Argument. He will begin, he says, with a *résumé* of the War in Heaven (past time), but it will not be shown directly just now.

Which action past over, the Poem hasts into the midst of things, presenting Satan with his Angels now fallen into Hell, describ'd here, not in the Center (for Heaven and Earth may be suppos'd

18 "Dante and Myth," *JHI,* X (1949), 501.

as not yet made, certainly not yet accurst) but in a place of utter
darknesse, fitliest call'd Chaos.

We are to see first a *place* of utter darkness, fitly located at
the bottom of the universe. The time/space distinction is
made interestingly after a few more lines, as Milton speaks
to the heavenly muse.

> Say first, for Heav'n hides nothing from thy view
> Nor the deep Tract of Hell, say first what cause
> Mov'd our Grand Parents in that happy State,
> Favour'd of Heav'n so highly, to fall off
> From their Creator . . . (i.27–31)

The rhetorical question is answered immediately by the poet
("Th' infernal Serpent; he it was . . . ") ; but how briefly!
In the space of twenty lines, we move swiftly back and forth
in time, to cover all the precedent causes of man's fall: *yes!*
Satan's rebellion, the War, his expulsion. At the end of this
rehearsal, we find ourselves at a place that is the very deepest
we are to encounter — not, in any way, the middle. Instead,
there is Satan rolling in the fiery gulf, thrice removed from
God and Heaven, the apex to which the poem will later rise.
In the lines quoted Milton, though he is urging the muse to
speak of what is *first* (in sequence, presumably), describes
her power as that of vision. She is able to *view* everything,
and Milton at once presents to us the whole extent of that
view, the physical stage of his action from Heaven to Hell.
We are given, too, some of the primary spatial-cum-moral
dimensions: "favour'd of Heav'n so *highly*, to *fall off*," and
deep Hell.

   Already, in the invocation a few lines before, the poet has
defined his own task geographically, through a punning
allusion; speaking to the muse "on the secret top" of a holy

mountain, about to embark on the adventure of his song,
Milton defines its path —

> That with no middle flight intends to soar
> Above th' *Aonian* Mount. (i.14–15)

He is referring to the three styles, "lofty, mean, or lowly," of
traditional rhetoric, intending us to understand that he is
aiming at the loftiest possible style and subject; but at the
same time, beginning to establish a mythic topography. On
these hills of rhetoric and myth — "the secret top Of *Oreb,*
or of *Sinai*," "*Sion* Hill," "th' *Aonian* Mount" — the poet
takes his stand, before pointing the paths we are to descend
into "the deep Tract of Hell," and later ascend to the gate of
Heaven. This is the first of a series of passages in which
Milton is to trace his own progress through the poem, too;
in each, he names the point *in space* that he and his great
argument have reached.

The structure of *Paradise Lost*, if we look down on all
this world at once, is a great inverted V; or, seen in three
dimensions, a mountain with its roots in Hell and its crown
in Heaven. We begin at the lowest point; we end at a point
not quite so low, but far below the heights to which we have
soared in the middle. Within this basic structure are a
number of smaller patterns where lesser ascents and descents
are followed. The whole is a great vision of rising and falling action; and in *Paradise Lost* the rise and fall are not only
emotional, moral, or social, as in tragedy, but literal and
topographical as well. Image and meaning are one.

Starting with Satan in his "proper place," Milton carries
him up through the first three books to Heaven's gate, then
to the sphere of the Sun, "alooff the vulgar Constellations
thick" (iii.577), and at last gently downward to Paradise,
the central tier of the stage, where Book IV and half of V

will take place. The lesser movements of Satan, down into Eden and up again over the mount of Paradise, have a local relevance though they are not part of the over-all design. Miss Mahood has said that "as we descend with Satan upon Paradise we experience the dreamer's fall as he is drawn into the vortex of sleep." [19] The tangled ascent of the hill that follows is part of the poem's sub-theme in which Satan is a hero on the perilous quest. Meanwhile, however, the major pattern is moving on beneath the surface. It rises into consciousness midway through Book V, as Adam questions Raphael concerning the War in Heaven, and the angel prepares to ascend, in narrative, above even the highest point of earth: "High matter thou injoinst me, O prime of men" (v. 563). He is about to tell of "what surmounts the reach Of human sense." Accordingly, we rise to the flaming Mount from which God speaks. The rest of this book, and the whole of the next, recount the War; at the end (the mid-point of the poem in space and duration), we have returned more or less to the *temporal* location of the opening: the time just after the fall of the rebel angels.[20] Now, however, we see it from above, stationed in Heaven. With the victorious angels, we participate in Christ's return, "Triumphant through mid Heav'n" (vi.589), into the courts of God.

In the proem to Book VII Milton, recalling his muse from her exalted seat, begins the downward journey that is to occupy, with a few intermissions, the poem's second half. "Descend from Heav'n *Urania*" —

[19] *Poetry and Humanism*, p. 181.

[20] This point is not affected, of course, by the change that Milton made in the second edition (1674), when the original ten books of *Paradise Lost* became twelve, the present Books VII and VIII, XI and XII, being divisions of what were single books in 1667. The poem still divides approximately in half at the end of the present Book VI, I–VI being about 300 lines longer than VII–XII; so Milton in fact made his design *more* symmetrical in the second edition, by allowing for an equal number of books before and after the mid-point.

> Up led by thee
> Into the Heav'n of Heav'ns I have presum'd,
> An Earthlie Guest, and drawn Empyreal Aire,
> Thy tempring; with like safetie guided down
> Return me to my Native Element.
>
> .   .   .   .   .
>
> Half yet remaines unsung, but narrower bound
> Within the visible Diurnal Spheare;
> Standing on Earth, not rapt above the Pole,
> More Safe I sing with mortal voice, unchang'd
> To hoarce or mute, though fall'n on evil dayes . . .
>
> (vii.12–16, 21–25)

In these lines, of course, Milton is speaking of his own life, as well as of his imaginative life as a Dantean pilgrim within the poem: his blindness, the evil tongues of his enemies, the barbarous dissonance of the Restoration. Nevertheless, structurally this speech parallels the one in Book III, where the poet was ascending the same height he is now descending, but moving then toward the light instead of away from it.

> Thee I re-visit now with bolder wing,
> Escap't the *Stygian* Pool, though long detain'd
> In that obscure sojourn, while in my flight
> Through utter and through middle darkness borne
> With other notes then to th' *Orphean* Lyre
> I sung of *Chaos* and *Eternal Night*,
> Taught by the heav'nly Muse to venture down
> The dark descent, and up to reascend,
> Though hard and rare; thee I revisit safe,
> And feel thy sovran vital Lamp. (iii.13–22)

The position here exactly matches that of Book VII, though here the future course is upward, there downward; we are about to launch into two books conducted on the plateau of unfallen Eden. From Book IX onward, the progress is steadily down, until, at the very end, we have descended with Adam and Eve to our own mundane world.

> In either hand the hastning Angel caught
> Our lingring Parents, and to th' Eastern Gate
> Led them direct, and down the Cliff as fast
> To the subjected Plaine. (xii.637–40)

This, then, is the main configuration of the poem: from deep Hell up to the Mount of God, and down again to the "subjected Plaine" of fallen earthly life. It contrasts with the pattern traced by a traditional mythic journey-theme, which takes either a linear form — quest toward a goal — or moves down into an underworld and thence returns. The scheme of *Paradise Lost* provides an arena *within which* these movements can take place, and do; but the major action reproduces the plan of the whole universe. This mountain-shaped structure has value-dimensions as well as physical ones; moral directions, whereby movement upward and downward toward light or darkness becomes meaningful, were a necessity for Milton's myth, and his architecture provides scope for advance or retreat as well as for repetitive action. The spiral design that appears if we look directly down on the mountain of the Creation from above is also, according to Jungian interpretation, a frequent dream motif, indicating "the process of development" or growth. "The centre or goal . . . signifies salvation in the proper sense of the word." [21]

Smaller structures within the large one are often seen in a similar way as rising and falling action. Of these, five are major sub-units. The first is the interlude in Heaven in Book III, where the whole Christian myth — man's fall and sub-

---

[21] C. G. Jung, *Psychology and Alchemy*, trans. R. F. C. Hull (New York, 1953), pp. 28–29.

sequent rise, redeemed by Christ — is related by God. It is
a break in the steady rise of the action carried by Satan; but
we do not lose sight of him. He is merely seen from a new
vantage-point. Milton uses shifts of perspective several times
to remind us that there are many places and points of view
that we must be simultaneously aware of; this is one of the
most striking, as the heroic Satan of the early books becomes
a small night-bird, barely visible from the flaming mount of
God.

> He then survey'd
> Hell and the Gulf between, and *Satan* there
> Coasting the wall of Heav'n on this side Night
> In the dun Air sublime, and ready now
> To stoop with wearied wings, and willing feet
> On the bare outside of this World. (iii.69–74)

This vision (which also includes "the Sanctities of Heaven"
and the Garden on earth) is the first of the great panoramic
views that punctuate *Paradise Lost* and show us the whole
sweep of Creation. Here Satan is precisely located, in relation to the other important places in the universe. The
pinpointing phrase, "on this side Night," translates what is
for us a temporal unit into a physical area, as it would look
if we could escape the limits of earthly knowledge.

The pattern's next figure is Eve's dream in Book V, where
the temptation, to ascend and "be thyself a Goddess," is
given graphically as an actual flight.

> Forthwith up to the Clouds
> With him I flew, and underneath beheld
> The Earth outstretcht immense, a prospect wide
> And various: wondring at my flight and change
> To this high exaltation; suddenly
> My Guide was gon, and I, me thought, sunk down,
> And fell asleep. (v.86–92)

This episode re-enacts Satan's flight to Heaven and his "sudden view Of all this World at once," and rehearses the aspiration that will precede the real Fall. Eve is allowed for a moment to "view all things at one view," like God.

A third interlude is the descent, in Book VII, of the Son "far into *Chaos*," the creation of the world, and the triumphal song "While the bright pomp ascended jubilant," which raises us again, for an instant, to the pinnacle of the epic structure. There is an inverted parallel in the bridge-building episode of Book X, when Sin and Death rise out of Chaos, meet Satan at the crossroads of the universe, and "right down to Paradise descend" (x.398). Finally, there is Adam's ascent of the hill, "of Paradise the highest," to see the kingdoms of the earth in a dream. His vision takes in all of human history, but though the episodes follow in sequence, the effect is static: a series of tableaux, not a cinema. From his perch,

> The Hemisphere of Earth in cleerest Ken
> Stretcht out to amplest reach of prospect lay. (xi.379–80)

On this stage, moralities and interludes are enacted, with Michael as chorus (later, as narrator). Adam, like Eve in Book V, is being granted for a moment participation in God's panoramic view from his "prospect high," or the vantage point of Christ at Heaven's gate, "from whence *Eden* and all the Coast in prospect lay" (x.89–90); time is a series of horizons, not a process lived through — the living will come soon enough. Michael sums up the wisdom gained by his pupil in words that compass the whole of the poem's universe. In accord with the gradual "spiritualization" of the theme toward the end, the drama has shifted from the physical universe to man's soul, and so the depths and heights are given different names, but they still resemble their analogues in the macrocosm:

> This having learnt, thou hast attaind the summe
> Of wisdom; hope no higher, though all the Starrs
> Thou knewst by name, all th' ethereal Powers,
> All secrets of the deep, all Natures works.
>
> .   .   .   .   .
>
> Let us descend now therefore from this top
> Of Speculation. (xii.575–89)

The descent is a prelude to the further descent into fallen human life.

One might add to these major incidents, the building-blocks of *Paradise Lost,* the last fall of Satan to Pandemonium in Book X, which completes the figure begun in Book I by returning him to his original level; he ends where he began. At this point, however, Satan's actions are no longer part of the poem's dominant movement; the focus has been transferred to Adam, and it is left to him to carry out the main pattern, while Satan falls symmetrically into the deep tract of Hell.

There are, in addition, several events that are meant to balance each other emotively and morally; Milton makes the connection by having them run literally along parallel lines, though they may be chronologically remote. Thus, Satan descends from Heaven's gate down to "the Worlds first Region," and Raphael follows on a parallel track in Book V. The two accounts are given in similar phrasing; the paths traversed are the same. Satan,

> Down right into the Worlds first Region throws
> His flight precipitant, and windes with ease
> Through the pure marble Air his oblique way
> Amongst innumerable Starrs, that shon
> Stars distant, but nigh hand seemd other Worlds.
> (iii.562–67)

Raphael, like him, pauses to look down at the world; then,

> Down thither prone in flight
> He speeds, and through the vast Ethereal Skie
> Sailes between worlds and worlds, with steddie wing
> Now on the polar windes, then with quick Fann
> Winnows the buxom Air. (v.266–70)

The image of the voyage among islands is used in both instances; each voyager at the end lights on a pinnacle, Niphates and "th' Eastern cliff of Paradise." The effect is at once to expand our attention toward the significant regions beyond Earth, and to contract it upon small, significant Paradise, as these spoke-like paths converge for their struggle.

Milton's balancing movements are not always parallel; toward the close of the poem, we catch sight of a crisscross pattern, a remote recurrence of the action and counteraction that have formed the main drama. Christ and Satan have been set off against each other throughout; a later episode of their antagonism is traced as Michael prophesies of the Resurrection:

> So spake this Oracle, then verifi'd
> When *Jesus* son of *Mary* second *Eve*
> Saw Satan fall like Lightning down from Heav'n,
> Prince of the Aire; then rising from his Grave
> Spoild Principalities and Powers, triumpht
> In open shew, and with ascension bright
> Captivity led captive through the Aire. (x.182–88)

It is interesting to compare this vision of the future, where Biblical phrases are combined to produce definite linear patterns, with Milton's statement of the same event in *Paradise Regained*. Christ speaks:

> Know'st thou not that my rising is thy fall,
> And my promotion will be thy destruction? (iii.201–202)

There is only the faintest shadow of the concrete in these lines; Jesus speaks "discursively" and paradoxically, in abstractions; and much of the poem, designed like medieval allegories for the instruction of a fallen race, is expressed in this sort of language. The brilliant hieroglyph of defeat and victory belongs to the mode of *Paradise Lost.*

"THIS PLACE TESTIFIES"

A diagram of the skeleton of *Paradise Lost* can give no idea of the extent to which we are made conscious, in the poem's verbal texture, of the structure's basic dimensions of depth and height, and the corresponding movements downward or upward. *Rise* and *raise, fall, high* and *height, low, deep* and *depth,* variations like *aspire* and *descend,* and the adverbs of direction, are repeated literally hundreds of times. It is, indeed, almost impossible to read through any ten lines of the poem without being aware of the way the compass is pointing. When a major direction is to be indicated, signposts accumulate: for example, as the fallen angels gather, "down cast and damp," at Satan's call, to have their courage "gently rais'd" by his "high words" (i.523 ff.). It is a turning-point, the beginning of a steady upward surge that will lead through Chaos to Eden. In a moment, the physical equivalent of "high words" appears, as the ensign is "up-rear'd" and "full high advanc't." The raised courage of the host is evident:

> At which the universal Host upsent
> A shout that tore Hells Concave, and beyond
> Frighted the Reign of *Chaos* and old Night. (i.541–43)

These reverberating lines have many emotional connotations; they also help to carry our attention upward into the next geographical region. In the succeeding march through Hell, banners and spears *rise,* flutes *raise* spirits. The total effect of the hundred-odd lines preceding Satan's first speech is of a vast ascent, both physical and spiritual. The process continues with the celebrated opening of Book II, a complex interplay of heights and depths.

> High on a Throne of Royal State, which far
> Outshon the wealth of *Ormus* and of *Ind,* . . .
> Satan exalted sat, by merit rais'd
> To that bad eminence; and from despair
> Thus high uplifted beyond hope, aspires
> Beyond thus high, insatiate to pursue
> Vain Warr with Heav'n, and by success untaught
> His proud imaginations thus displaid.
> Powers and Dominions, Deities of Heav'n,
> For since no deep within her gulf can hold
> Immortal vigor, though opprest and fall'n,
> I give not Heav'n for lost. From this descent
> Celestial vertues rising, will appear
> More glorious and more dread then from no fall. (ii.1–16)

The memory of the fall is still keen, but the thrust of the passage is up toward the heights. Satan's manipulation of *rise* and *fall* in the last lines form, too, a kind of parody of the *felix culpa,* the fortunate fall in which God miraculously reverses the ordinary implications of his universal structure so that a descent becomes really the first step in an ascent. Satan's words — "from this descent celestial vertues rising" — describe what happens to man, but only through God's grace; Satan's own hope of achieving it is given the lie in Book X, where a more abject fall awaits him.

Milton's directional words habitually mingle literal and what we should call figurative meanings. When Satan speaks of "this descent," he refers to an actual fall; but the same word can indicate a spiritual movement. Good "descends" from Heaven (vii.513); we have *seen* high Heaven, looked down from its height, and so this abstract, figurative descent acquires a pictorial shadow. So it is throughout *Paradise Lost:* we do not seek to draw lines between images and qualities, literal and metaphorical speech. Although Milton left allegory behind when he wrote the poem, moving "from shadowie Types to Truth" (xii.303), the qualities that inhabit allegories receive new incarnations in the persons and places of the epic, or find their old incarnations in its mythical shapes. The concrete vision of myth admits no disembodied abstractions. "The mythical *form of thought*, which attaches all qualities and activities, all states and relations to a solid foundation, leads to . . . a kind of materialization of spiritual contents." [22] Thus, qualities of an ideal humanity are "all summ'd up in Man" as Milton portrays him. He is "with native Honour clad"; in the persons of Adam and Eve,

> The image of thir glorious Maker shon,
> Truth, wisdome, Sanctitude severe and pure. (iv.292–93)

And Adam says of Eve, "Greatness of mind and nobleness thir seat Build in her loveliest" (viii.557–58). Milton's picture of unfallen man accords with the metaphysic of the *Christian Doctrine*, where he is unusually, even heretically, explicit in his denial of dualism.

Man is a living being, intrinsically and properly one and individual, not compound or separable, not, according to the common opinion, made up and framed of two distinct and different natures, as of soul and body, [but] . . . the whole man is soul, and the soul man, that is to say, a body, or substance individual, animated, sensitive, and rational.[23]

[22] Cassirer, *Mythical Thought,* p. 55.
[23] I, vii. *SM,* p. 979.

At the Fall of Man, the perfect unity of human nature was damaged, though not completely destroyed. Milton's conviction that qualities are ideally inseparable from objects could be carried effectively into his picture of ideal nature and human nature in *Paradise Lost*, and into the map of his living cosmos. Satan approaching the Garden "saw undelighted all delight" (iv.287); *delight* is given its very body in Milton's Eden.

Not only are these abstractions solid; they are potent. Satan, thinking of his fall, recalls that

Pride and worse Ambition threw me down
Warring in Heav'n against Heav'ns matchless King. (iv.40–41)

Here evil "intercepts" (v.871); Beauty "disarms" enmity (ix.465). Even when they are not definitely embodied, Milton's qualities are concretely felt as power; and in myth, such potency has as much "reality" as physical mass: "Whatever is capable of affecting mind, feeling, or will has thereby established its undoubted reality." [24] The tiers of Milton's stage are areas of power which is just as objective as physical force because it affects mind and will. If "abstractions" become concrete in a world of myth, concrete beings also are "spiritualized," endowed with invisible but effective power. Mere visibility or tangibility is not an indispensable criterion of reality; *effect* is what matters.

Paradise Lost is a poem of forces, of constant pressure on mind, feeling, and will. The poetry makes us experience these pressures by manifesting their upward thrust or downward drag, the direction of their movement within Milton's universe. "High thoughts," "high words," "high matter" propel the actors upward; recurrent falls attest to the power

[24] Henri and H. A. Frankfort, "Myth and Reality," in Henri Frankfort et al., *The Intellectual Adventure of Ancient Man* (Chicago, 1946), p. 11.

of "lower" impulses. The spiritual forces at work in the action, though they may be invisible to mortal sight, can be given a degree of unseen but physical reality, by being located in the poem's imaginative structure. The poetic problem of projecting these realities into a form that would faithfully reflect their peculiar nature was considerable. They could not be described in imagery, for they were imageless; in any case, Milton's use of metaphor was limited by his mythic subject, which dictated a more or less "literal" transcription. The construction of a plan in which physical areas had moral meaning solved this problem, making it possible to characterize immaterial forces by telling where they lived and where they went; it is a method unique in *Paradise Lost,* managed with beautiful tact by Milton. The firm foundation of the poem's geography gives a physical dimension to all the action played out against it; and our "spatial" awareness of this geography is constantly renewed — sometimes directly, in a panoramic vision or a topographical roll call, sometimes in the poem's texture, by "pointing" words. "The Heav'ns wide Circuit," the "Edifice" of the "great Architect," assumes a reality so solid and present, that it can confer a similar reality on all the Creation within.

Even more important, in this mythic poem, than the dynamic orientation of moral action, is the establishment of moral *areas,* the points of relation for that action. In the scheme of Milton's universe, simultaneously physical and spiritual, the word *place* stands not only for spatial location, but includes the semi-figurative uses made explicit in phrases like "to know one's place" or "high place" — position in a scale social, metaphysical, or religious. As Raphael describes the scale of nature, *place* indicates at once spiritual and geographical estate —

> But more refin'd, more spiritous, and pure,
> As neerer to him plac't or neerer tending. (v.475–76)

The place inhabited by a creature gives the key to its moral status, because moral values inhere in places; the word itself comes to take on the suggestion of *proper* place: "Fell with his flaming Legions through the Deep Into his place" (vii.134–35); or, "Th' event was dire, As this place testifies," says Satan in Hell (i.624–25). Place testifies again when the sentence on the serpent alters his position to accord with his act: "Upon thy Belly groveling thou shalt goe" (x.177). The idea that man's sin was a *fall* is an almost too obvious instance of the venerable habit of mind that equates physical and moral place. As a result of this equation, the "mixing" of places can have serious moral consequences. When Adam says of Eve, "All higher knowledge in her presence falls Degraded" (viii.551–52), he is betraying the fatal mote in his eye that causes him to mistake the appointed order of things; the higher falls, and other falls inevitably follow. Milton makes it clear that Adam has been placed by God above Eve, and his sin is a retreat from his proper place.

> To her
> Thou did'st resigne thy Manhood, and the Place
> Wherein God set thee above her made of thee. (x.147–49)

This denial of place is followed by expulsion from the happy place of Paradise, and a descent to the "subjected Plaine," one step closer to Chaos where "length, breadth, and highth, And time and place are lost" (ii.893–94).[25]

---

25 Milton's emphasis on place can be justified mythologically; to "primitive" minds place, not time, was the crucial form of perception. Cassirer writes *(Mythical Thought,* p. 92): "For mythical thinking the relation between what a thing 'is' and the place in which it is situated is never purely external and

Milton's treatment of place as a moral dimension receives its most subtle modulations in his tracing of the fortunes of Satan. For him, high on his throne in Pandemonium, physical and spiritual eminences merge, and he sees himself on a pinnacle appropriate to his worth, defying God: "whom the highest place exposes Formost" (ii.27–28). This is an attempt to establish his own hierarchy; his dependence on Heaven, even in sin, is shown by his reiteration of its equation between external and internal value. Satan's other claims on place are bound up with his experience of change, and the passage of time that has brought change about; he clings to place — that is, permanence — in an attempt to deny that he is subject to time's pressure. Although he has been enduring change ever since his first wound in Heaven ("then *Satan* first knew pain"), he boasts of being changeless. This is a way of claiming that he is, for all practical purposes, still in Heaven; that the essential qualities of Heaven are his to carry about with him. He professes, notoriously, to be

> One who brings
> A mind not to be chang'd by Place or Time.
> The mind is its own place, and in it self
> Can make a Heav'n of Hell, a Hell of Heav'n. (i.252–55)

This assertion has been admired as a profound truth; but Milton did not put truth, except in the guise of irony, in the Devil's mouth, and in the large context of *Paradise Lost* it is not true. Rather, it is a specious denial by Satan of his fall: the rejection of time is a rejection of change, and a

---

accidental; the place is itself a part of the thing's being, and the place confers very special ties upon the thing."

Again, "districts in space, direction (the points of the compass), have mysterious significance" for primitive thinkers, according to Lucien Lévy-Bruhl. *How Natives Think,* trans. Lilian A. Clare (New York, 1926), p. 40.

claim to be still a denizen of changeless Heaven. It is disproved in the poem's later movements: in the roll call of Book I, recounting the dreadful metamorphoses of the fallen angels, and in Satan's own brutal change in Book X. The assertion reaffirms the self-sufficiency that led Satan to his rebellion; in making it, he is cutting himself off from the vital forces that permeate the universe. "The mind is its own place" separates mind from its external surroundings — a state of affairs impossible in Heaven or in unfallen Paradise, where spirit and flesh, surface and depth, are in harmony. Satan's remark is an ominous forecast of a situation that we know too well ourselves: the hostility of reality and appearance. The dissonance between inner and outer being is presented explicitly in his first speech, where the attitude toward change appears suggestively:

> Yet not for those
> Nor what the Potent Victor in his rage
> Can else inflict do I repent or change,
> Though chang'd in outward lustre. (i.94–97)

He fails to realize that change in outward lustre signifies a moral change that has already taken place, in a world obedient still to the simple design of creation where, in Spenser's neo-Platonic phrase, "all that fair is, is by nature good." The angel Zephon, Satan's captor, reveals the vanity of the claim: "think not, revolted Spirit, thy shape the same" —

> Thou resembl'st now
> Thy sin and place of doom obscure and foule. (iv.839–40)

Satan's contempt of "outward lustre" does point, however, to a time when he will actually be able to conceal malice under

a fair show that no longer reflects an inward fairness; the
bitter torment of dissimulation racks the world of the fallen,
as he recognizes in a rare moment of insight:

> While they adore me on the Throne of Hell,
> With Diadem and Scepter high advanc't
> The lower still I fall, onely supream
> In miserie. (iv.89–92)

"The mind is its own place" has here acquired a terrible and
unexpected meaning.

Satan's arguments about place have, therefore, a kind of
truth — though it is a truth that recoils on the speaker and
proves itself in a direction opposite from the one intended.
As Milton observes,

> within him Hell
> He brings, and round about him, nor from Hell
> One step no more then from himself can fly
> By change of place. (iv.20–23)

This is the dreadful truth that Satan himself admits a few
lines later. His isolation has been successful. He is, indeed,
no more to be changed by place; he is immune to the enormous bliss of Eden, untouched by the sun's rays that im-
part light to all. Instead, he has become capable himself of
changing the place in which he is: the shadow of Hell falls
on the paradisal brightness where he moves. The desolating
futility of his cry to God can only be understood in the context of his former claims:

> O then at last relent: is there no place
> Left for Repentance, none for Pardon left? (iv.79–80)

But he has already boasted himself unchanged by place; the

place of repentance, the place of pardon, the place of Paradise, and the powers that live there, are being made inaccessible to him by his own act. He confesses as much when
the sight of Eden's joys quickens his sense of loss: "but I in
none of these Find place or refuge" (ix.118–19). His doom
is now that he *cannot* change his place.

THE MOVING IMAGE OF ETERNITY

The structure of *Paradise Lost,* the enormous ascending
and descending mountain, is not accidental or eccentric; it
is built on the idea of hierarchy that was an integral part of
the Christian myth, the visible image of God's eternal plan.
The incorporation of temporal processes into this timeless
structure is one of the most interesting achievements of the
poet who set out in his poem to span the whole of human
history.

Time is, of course, a function of all created beings because they, unlike their Creator, the Unmoved Mover, live
by motion, which is measured by time. Milton had affirmed
that time is "the measure of motion," [26] and the idea is repeated in *Paradise Lost.*

> For Time, though in Eternitie, appli'd
> To motion, measures all things durable
> By present, past, and future. (v.580–82)

The higher in the scale of nature a being is, the more "immediate" are its motions and, therefore, the less subject to
time. Of Christ's journey to Eden, Milton writes:

Down he descended strait; the speed of Gods
Time counts not, though with swiftest minutes wing'd. (x.90–91)

26 *Christian Doctrine,* I, vii. *SM,* p. 978.

Although unfallen man was much less bound to discourse and "process" than his descendants, time was still necessary.

> Immediate are the Acts of God, more swift
> Then time or motion, but to human ears
> Cannot without process of speech be told. (vii.176–78)

Time in the unfallen world, nevertheless, differs from our endless linear time, and can be distinguished by the kind of motion it measures. In Heaven, it seems to exist chiefly to pursue the circles of the angelic dance "about the sacred Hill." A similar pattern is established for men, at the creation of day and night.

> Let them be for Signes,
> For Seasons, and for Days, and circling Years. (vii.341–42)

Time is the vehicle of change; but change, too, can be of more than one kind. In Heaven and Paradise, it is a sweet variety; Raphael tells Adam that evening and morning provide the angels with "change delectable," and Milton elaborates the picture in a later book.

> There is a Cave
> Within the Mount of God, fast by his Throne,
> Where light and darkness in perpetual round
> Lodge and dislodge by turns, which makes through Heav'n
> Grateful vicissitude, like Day and Night. (vi.4–8)

This change is limited and bound by recurrence; it is a cycle, like the shepherds' time in *Lycidas,* where nothing is ever lost, but is merely located at a different point on an immense circle, "the Wheele of Day and Night." Adam and Eve stand at the still point of the turning world, watching it revolve in a "Perpetual Circle," assured that it will continue to revolve. The image of the spinning top with a still center is explicit in Raphael's outline of the alternative theories of celestial motion; peace and permanence emerge through the tone of the descriptions, no matter which is chosen.

> Whether the Sun predominant in Heav'n
> Rise on the Earth, or Earth rise on the Sun,
> Hee from the East his flaming rode begin,
> Or Shee from West her silent course advance
> With inoffensive pace that spinning sleeps
> On her soft Axle, while she paces Eev'n,
> And bears thee soft with the smooth Air along. (viii.160–66)

The *length* of time becomes unimportant in such a world. So, for example, we are not told exactly the number of hours or days that elapse between the creation of man and Raphael's visit, but we are given, on many different occasions, a picture of the wheeling, steady heavens.

> Those have thir course to finish, round the Earth,
> By morrow Eevning, and from Land to Land
> In order, though to Nations yet unborn,
> Ministring light prepar'd, they set and rise. (iv.661–64)

The phases of the moon provide a fine example of recurrence, and Uriel's discourse on them is full of rhythmic motion.

> Her monthly round
> Still ending, still renewing through mid Heav'n,
> With borrowd light her countenance triform
> Hence fills and empties to enlighten the Earth,
> And in her pale dominion checks the night. (iii.728–32)

The gigantic visions through space are famous, and almost always they reveal the majestic mechanisms of an orderly perpetual motion. Some of Milton's grandest poetry is spent in explaining them: the "mazes intricate" in Book V, the discussions of Adam and Raphael in Book VIII, and the reshaping of this order to "Synod unbenigne" in Book X where time becomes a sickness. The expense is not in vain; for these revelations of cosmic order reassure us that nature's holy plan is not only reliable, but visible; we are made aware that, as the angels see it, it is a wholly articulate pattern in the immensities of space.

In spite of his view that measurement is time's function, Milton sometimes gives motion in terms of space; for example, "Nine times the Space that measures Day and Night" (i.50), or, as Satan advances among the stars:

> They as they move
> Thir Starry dance in numbers that compute
> Days, months, and years. (iii.579–81)

Here temporal units become spatial, and a day is only a measure in the dance. Again, as an angel descends —

> Thither came *Uriel,* gliding through the Eeven
> On a Sun beam, swift as a shooting Starr
> In *Autumn* thwarts the night, when vapors fir'd
> Impress the Air, and shews the Mariner
> From what point of his Compass to beware
> Impetuous winds. (iv.555–60)

This was one of the passages that enraged Bentley, whose remark on it is nevertheless pertinent.

I never heard but here, that the *Evening* was a Place or Space to *glide* through. Evening implies Time, and he might with equal propriety say, *Came gliding through Six a clock.*[27]

Whether or not it was always conscious, Milton experienced the world of his epic architecturally, in terms of mass and

[27] *Milton's Paradise Lost. A New Edition,* ed. Richard Bentley (London, 1732), p. 126.

space. The modulation of time into spatial effects, which Bentley precisely though disapprovingly describes, is the result. The simile expands the implication, with the wonderful spatial (and probably kinesthetic) verb *thwarts,* and the reference to the points of the compass. *Thwarts,* too, reminds us of Milton's cosmic war where darkness is thwarted by light.

The finest of all the transformations of time in Eden takes place when its changing sameness is re-enacted in Eve's beautiful iterative speech to Adam, "With thee conversing I forget all time" (iv.639 ff.). Adam *is* Eden, in a very real sense, for Eve; he is what gives Paradise its special splendor. "Thou to mee Art all things under Heav'n, all places thou" (xii.617–18). In her communion with him, the constancy of Paradise, the sweetness and benevolence underlying all its superficial changes, reach their culmination: "All seasons and thir change, all please alike." The repetition, almost word for word, of her speech, enacts a timeless recurrence that is confirmed both in the sense of the words and in Milton's picture of Paradise as a whole.

In deliberate contrast to this peace, the denizens of Hell are obsessed with time and the heavy change of their condition. In this part of the poem, no less than in the central section, Milton steadily maintains his massive spatial frame, pointing the location of each event. But the actors can no longer see *sub specie aeternitatis.* Their sense of loss is reflected in the perpetual contrasts between present misery and a happy past. The frequency of Milton's references to change in *Paradise Lost* points to a convenient non-temporal way of indicating the passage of time: comparison and contrast. Such comparisons naturally thicken at the beginning and end of the poem, starting with the first words spoken by Satan: "If thou beest he; but O how fall'n! how chang'd" (i.84). Milton has just described Hell, negatively:

> As far remov'd from God and light of Heav'n
> As from the Center thrice to th' utmost Pole.
> O how unlike the place from whence they fell! (i.73–75)

The typically "geometrical" statement of relationships [28] is followed by a key phrase destined to resound through Satan's consciousness and give us the very note of his fate: "O how unlike." It is repeated at Adam and Eve's first act after their fall; covering their shame, they are "O how unlike To that first naked Glorie" (ix.1114–15). With the fall of angels and men, comparison — like contention and ambiguity, an aspect of dangerous doubleness — enters the world; and this comparison is necessarily made between *before* and *after*, *then* and *now*, as Satan makes it: "Warriers, the Flowr of Heav'n, once yours, now lost." (i.316) He observes them gathering dejectedly, "far other once beheld in bliss" (i.607). Satan's awareness of time reaches a climax when the sight of Paradise presses contrast on him.

>   Now conscience wakes despair
> That slumberd, wakes the bitter memorie
> Of what he was, what is, and what must be
> Worse; of worse deeds worse sufferings must ensue. (iv.23–26)

He addresses the sun,

>   To tell thee how I hate thy beams
> That bring to my remembrance from what state
> I fell, how glorious once above thy Spheare. (iv.37–39)

The natural nostalgia of the fallen angels enables Milton to

---

28 B. A. Wright has explained that Milton's phrase is not to be taken literally: "'thrice' is of course an intensive, or rather indefinitely extensive, not a computative expression," and, "in effect," a simile. The important word in this description is *extensive*. "Masson's Diagram of Milton's Spaces," *RES*, XXI (1945), 43.

present a continuous counterpoint between past and future that merges with the greater contrast and conflict between his major forces. The angels' temporal measurements, *once* and *now*, become, in the perspective of the whole, simply another way of stating the antagonism between Heaven and Hell; time is absorbed into the visible dramatic structure.

The angels' awareness of time's awful pressure stretches into the future as well, a future "without hope of end" (ii. 89), though Belial sees a glimmer through the mist of time:

> This horror will grow milde, this darkness light,
> Besides what hope the never-ending flight
> Of future days may bring, what chance, what change
> Worth waiting. (ii.220–23)

But the very idea of chance and change produced by the flight of days is alien to the chanceless, changeless heavens; the idea of waiting itself indicates that Belial has left behind the country of fulfilment, where each moment sums up the whole of bliss in a passionate immediacy. An echo of this speech comes toward the end of the poem, when the divine voice is heard calling to the fallen Adam: "what change Absents thee, or what chance detains?" (x.107–8). The possibility of accident, the inevitability of change, elements of an unknowable future, are products of the Fall. Illusion and futility, too, are inevitable results of the lapse into an uncertain time-ridden existence: a shrouded future, stretching into a dark realm of possibility, provides a foundation for impossible dreams, like that of the fallen angels,

> To found this nether Empire, which might rise
> By pollicy, and long process of time,
> In emulation opposite to Heav'n. (ii.295–98)

The futility of this is exposed in the next books, where we

read: "Immediate are the Acts of God, more swift Then time . . ." (vii.176–77).

Satan brings the poison of time with him into Paradise, and the first breath of impermanence touches it as he speaks:

> Live while ye may,
> Yet happie pair; enjoy, till I return,
> Short pleasures, for long woes are to succeed. (iv.533–35)

Time's shadow falls most noticeably over the final books of the epic. Before the Fall, it faithfully restored each well loved object to the light of day, but now it can swallow them up in its dark backward. Adam speaks wearily to Eve the words that will be echoed by millions of their descendants: "But past who can recall, or don undoe?" (ix.926). In the last books, too, we begin to be aware of receding planes within the framework which, though still observed in panorama from the top of a mountain, "stretcht out to amplest reach of prospect," seem to carry the eye away to a point outside the main system of the mythical surface. Milton set out to include in his poem all history, and even a hint of the end of history, but these could not be allowed to interfere with the great rising/falling structure. So we see them as tiny retracings in the far distance, or diminished replicas of what we have already seen. The events of history are recognizable, being shaped from the same mould as the main action; but they are distorted by the changes of time and sin, and less sharply drawn. Thus, the rising of the Evening Star, "Loves Harbinger," on the amours of the Sethites (xi.585 ff.) is almost a parody of the sensuously rich passage in Book VIII on the nuptial bower of Eden, but it is roughly blocked in, a painted stage-set rather than a living scene.

Adam's perspective into history is followed by the brief close of *Paradise Lost* where we, with fallen man, are allowed a final glimpse of the familiar stage. It is carefully composed: at one side, Adam and the angel on their mount, on the opposite hill, the bright array of the cherubim. The last sixty lines form a steady descending action, first from one hill, then from the other, with the image of the misty marsh to indicate the lowness of the central ground. The last definite, brilliant vision of the place of Paradise — the cliff, the flaming brand, the gate — is succeeded by the width and vagueness of the future:

> The World was all before them, where to choose
> Thir place of rest, and Providence thir guide. (xii.646–47)

The trustworthy structured universe is left behind for search, the discovery of unknown places in the long process of time.

COMPLEX WORDS

A final medium for "retrospection and anticipation" is provided by Milton's use of repeated phrases and systems of "key words" or images. Such repetitions are one of the most pervasive unifying forces in the poem, though they do not yield their full effect at a first reading. An awareness of the correspondences in Milton's poetic world is one of the greatest pleasures to be gained by rereading *Paradise Lost,* and it explains, in large part, why the poem improves with familiarity. The precision of the machinery set in motion, the wheels within wheels of allusion, forecast, and echo, cannot be guessed beforehand. Book I cannot be properly read until we are acquainted with Book XII, though the last book has grown from seeds sown in the first.

The method can fairly be called structural, since it is one of Milton's major tools in the translation of his fable from a chronological to an architectural idiom. By freeing his material from the limits of chronology, Milton could concentrate on emotional relationships and bring together incidents or images to shed light on each other. One way of effecting this was to recall or anticipate words and symbols whenever the associations clustering round them were relevant to the context. The most important event in a series could be placed at a structural key-point, regardless of its "actual" chronological position. The place of an incident in the reader's experience is thus determined in *Paradise Lost* not by its temporal weight, but by its mythical charge, demanding that it appear and reappear in several of the expanding circles raying out from the initial statement. The epic practice of linguistic formulas provided, of course, a precedent for Milton's repetitive diction; but, as always, convention became innovation as it was brought into harmony with the overriding demands of his subject. In the genre to which *Paradise Lost* belongs, variously called "secondary" or "literary" epic, the old technique of stock phrases, practiced by the authors of "primary" epic, was dying out as the conditions of oral poetry that produced it came to an end. But a long poem remains a long poem for the recipient, whether listener or reader, and so, although bardic precedent did not weigh very heavily upon the author of a literary epic, regard for his audience might demand that he retain its verbal conventions. Milton's limited, weighted vocabulary functions, though more intensely, in much the same way that the formulas of Homer and the Anglo-Saxon poets worked for their listeners. It helps us to hold the whole sweep of the poem firmly in mind, recalling to us constantly the essential elements in its foundation. Milton's repetitions in language are, of course, much more deliberately controlled than those of the old epic poets, more intricately related to the poem's structure as well as its texture. They cannot, in fact, be called formulas at all, in the strict classical sense. Scholars have pointed out that the appearance of identical phrases in the Homeric epics was governed by a criterion of "usefulness" for the meter and the immediate context of meaning. The "true" formula is defined as "a group of words which is regularly employed under the same metrical conditions to express a given essential idea." As this writer goes on to explain, "When the element of usefulness is lacking, one does not have a formula but a repeated phrase which has been knowingly brought into the verse for some special effect." [29] Certainly, practical considerations sometimes govern the repeated phrases of *Paradise Lost,* but generally Milton was striving for those "special effects" that go beyond "usefulness," and demand a more flexible manipulation of language than any permitted by traditional formulas.

The effects that support the poem's structure through the use of repetitive linguistic forms can be observed in microcosm in the first three and a half lines of *Paradise Lost.* Here Milton is laying the groundwork, through at least four continuing systems of words, ideas, and images, for future recognitions that will show "future" to be simply a familiar configuration on the surface of uniform mythical life.

> Of Mans First Disobedience, and the Fruit
> Of that Forbidden Tree, whose mortal tast
> Brought Death into the World, and all our woe,
> With loss of *Eden* . . . (i.1–4)

The tree itself is one of the poem's major icons; Death is a character, of whom the word *mortal* reminds us some twenty times at crucial points. *Fruit* and *woe* are key words to which critical associations are attached in the course of the poem;

---

[29] Milman Parry, "Studies in the Epic Technique of Oral Verse-Making," *Harvard Studies in Classical Philology,* XLI (1930), 80–81.

they are also linked, syntactically and logically, to each other, since the woe of change and loss is one of the fruits of the forbidden tree.

The use of the phrase "all our woe" as a *leitmotiv* in *Paradise Lost,* recurring in a number of instances "in the same prominent place in the meter," has been discussed by E. E. Stoll,[30] whose example comes from Book IX: "the Tree Of prohibition, root of all our woe" (ix.644–45). The echoed cadence, here and elsewhere, is of some importance, since poets certainly "think" in rhythms and wordless tunes very often, and the coincidence of word and cadence imposes recollection on an alert reader as well. Also important is the logical link between *tree* and its fruit, *woe,* the causal link being compressed into the *root* image, one of Milton's characteristic reinforcing ambiguities, drawing sustenance from two sources for one central meaning. The same logic was found in lines 1–3, above; and the idea of woe as a consequence or "fruit" is stressed throughout. In Book II Sin's "fatal key" is "Sad instrument of all our woe" (ii.872); and later, Eve prays that guilt may light "On me, sole cause to thee of all this woe" (x.935). In the fall of this line there is, perhaps, another echo: "all that pain" of Ceres seeking Proserpina. Adam, like Ceres, must follow his fallen Eve "through the world" and even into "a lower world." Again, Satan is imagined by Adam as he "seeks to work us woe and shame" (ix.255), and in the next book the woe and shame fall elsewhere as the fallen angels see a whole grove of trees in hallucination:

> For one forbidden Tree a multitude
> Now ris'n, to work them furder woe and shame. (x.554–55)

[30] "Time and Space in Milton," *From Shakespeare to Joyce* (New York, 1944), p. 424.

In the Prologue to the ninth book, the poet speaks of the judgment "That brought into this World a world of woe" (ix.11); and this phrase is itself an echo of an echo, God's speech in Book VIII, where the associations of the opening lines are recombined in variation:

> The day thou eat'st thereof, my sole command
> Transgrest, inevitably thou shalt dye;
> From that day mortal, and this happie State
> Shalt loose, expell'd from hence into a World
> Of woe and sorrow. (viii.329–33)

In the passages just picked out, crucial moments from four books of the epic have been joined to the ominous initiatory lines. As the key turns to release Satan from his prison (through gates never to be closed until the Last Judgment); as God pronounces the fatal prohibition; as Milton, foreseeing the catastrophe, changes "these notes to tragic"; as Eve is led to the Tree; as the full awareness of her sin darkens her consciousness; as woe overtakes the original sinners in Hell — at each of these points, another knot of the pattern is tied, and a network of implication is spread over the poem. There are, besides, other reverberations of *woe,* most of them centering on the fallen angels in Book II, Satan's entry into Paradise in Book IV, and the Fall itself in IX and X. A poignant instance comes when the angels in Hell approach Lethe,

> And wish and struggle, as they pass, to reach
> The tempting stream, with one small drop to loose
> In sweet forgetfulness all pain and woe. (ii.606–608)

Milton's "classical" Hell has proleptic force in *Paradise Lost* as a forecast of the woes of humanity; here it both echoes line 3 and anticipates the "sense of endless woes" (x.754) that waits at the end.

If this "network" produced by the word *woe* seems frail, we must remember that its strength is multiplied a hundred-fold when it is combined with all the similar nets cast by Milton. For example, he counterbalances the warnings of woe as a forbidden fruit by a reminder of other fruits that will spring from the *felix culpa*. Our first picture of Adam and Eve "reaping immortal fruits of joy and love" in Paradise (iii.67) is followed by a shadow of disaster, but also of redemption and the end of the world. After the Last Judgment, the just will dwell in a new Paradise:

> And after all thir tribulations long
> See golden days, fruitful of golden deeds,
> With Joy and Love triumphing, and fair Truth. (iii.336–38)

As the poem ends, Adam is shown a vision of the same new world:

> Founded in righteousness and peace and love,
> To bring forth fruits Joy and eternal Bliss. (xii.550–51)

The immediate "fruits" of God's pity for fallen man have already been accepted in Heaven, at the Son's intercession:

> See Father, what first fruits on Earth are sprung
> From thy implanted Grace in Man, these Sighs
> And Prayers. (xi.20–22)

A similar chain of references to the Tree itself may be pursued; and there is another intricate pattern in Milton's variations on the word *mortal*, through which some of the major episodes in the career of Death are projected. The apparently conventional phrase of line 3 — "brought Death into the World" — is literally developed in Book X where a real Death is seen entering a fallen world; before and after this incident, a sequence of undertones in *mortal* strengthens the concept and makes its threatening presence pervasive. Every incident, every speech, almost every phrase of *Paradise Lost* casts light back and ahead to illuminate past and future so that we are made aware of the entire myth at once. The relatively small vocabulary used in the poem means that there is necessarily a high frequency of repeated words and phrases which gather significance as they go along and reinforce, even while they borrow strength from, our familiarity with the story.

point of technique

The same effect is achieved on a larger scale when Milton arranges patterns of images whose associations interact to help knit together the mythic meaning. James Whaler has discussed this "proleptic imagery" in his article on Milton's similes.[31] It is one of the poet's techniques for "unfolding what is already known," a kind of substitute in reverse for suspense. In many instances, our appreciation and insight depend as much on "retrospection" as on anticipation; a final incident may recapitulate and clarify a whole preceding series, once more contradicting the usually past-to-future progress of ordinary narrative. An example is a group of "destruction" images clustering around Satan and his works, which may be said to end with the much-admired passage in Book XI on the fate of Paradise after the Flood. Many readers have felt the reverberating force of these lines; it is not always recognized that some of the force is cumulative, gathered and echoed from a carefully-laid train in earlier books.

> all fountaines of the Deep
> Broke up, shall heave the Ocean to usurp
> Beyond all bounds, till inundation rise
> Above the highest Hills: then shall this Mount

[31] "The Miltonic Simile," *PMLA*, XLVI (1931), 1034–74.

Of Paradise by might of Waves be moovd
Out of his place, pushd by the horned floud,
With all his verdure spoil'd, and Trees adrift
Down the great River to the op'ning Gulf,
And there take root an Iland salt and bare,
The haunt of Seales and Orcs, and Sea-mews clang. (xi.826–35)

The passage has been singled out as an instance of Milton's "primitive awe of wild nature," [32] and so it is; but the awe is not of a mysterious unknown force. Milton is telling us how this state of affairs came to be; it is a partial reversion to the most primeval wilderness of all, from which Creation sprang — Chaos, the "abortive Gulf" wider than the Gulf that now swallows Paradise. The lines therefore look back to the anarchic waves of Book II, and also make a parallel in nature to the chaotic disorder in the minds of fallen Adam and Eve. The spoiled verdure, too, we have met before, in the singed pines of Book I, though this time water, not fire, has wrought destruction; and the bare salt island is a final instance of Milton's primary symbol for evil, barrenness. Analogues to this scene come at a number of critical points in the poem, and are caused by similar forces. When Satan battles with Abdiel, he is staggered by a blow —

          as if on Earth
Winds under ground or waters forcing way
Sidelong, had push't a Mountain from his seat
Half sunk with all his Pines. (vi.195–98)

The mountain pushed by the flood, the ruined trees, forecast the details of the later passage. In Book I, the same image of an uprooted hill appears as Milton describes the scorched earth of Hell.

32 E. M. W. Tillyard, *The Miltonic Setting* (Cambridge, 1938), p. 54.

And such appear'd in hue, as when the force
Of subterranean wind transports a Hill
Torn from *Pelorus* or the shatter'd side
Of thundring *Aetna*. (i.230–33)

There is a similar effect in a simile introducing the war-games in Hell, including two legendary examples.

Others with vast *Typhoean* rage more fell
Rend up both Rocks and Hills, and ride the Air
In whirlwind; Hell scarce holds the wilde uproar.
As when *Alcides* from *Oechalia* Crown'd
With conquest, felt th' envenom'd robe, and tore
Through pain up by the roots *Thessalian* Pines . . .
(ii.539–44)

Hercules is, to be sure, a diminished modern instance, closer to the battling gods of Hesiod, or to Virgil's warriors; he is not so much a metaphorical equivalent of Hell's denizens, as a faint reflection of them caught in the mirror of classical mythology. Behind these examples from later stories can be heard faint rumblings from the geological dislocations of prehistory revealed by Milton.

The most memorable appearance of torn hills in *Paradise Lost* occurs, of course, at the crisis of the War in Heaven.

From thir foundations loosning to and fro
They pluckt the seated Hills with all thir load,
Rocks, Waters, Woods . . .
The bottom of the Mountains upward turn'd. (vi.643–49)

Like phrasing and significance are visible in the picture of Chaos before the Creation; the War, indeed, was a violation of Heaven by Chaos. Milton's image perhaps owes something to the raging seas of the first book of the *Aeneid,* but the end of this passage is purely Christian, as outrageous nature is tamed.

> They view'd the vast immeasurable Abyss
> Outrageous as a Sea, dark, wasteful, wilde,
> Up from the bottom turn'd by furious windes
> And surging waves, as Mountains to assault
> Heav'ns highth, and with the Center mix the Pole.
>   Silence, ye troubl'd waves, and thou Deep, peace,
> Said then th' Omnific Word, your discord end. (vii.211–16)

The reversion to Chaos after the Fall is shown in two similes
in Book X, where violence once more assaults nature and
the Abyss rages untamed, until part of it is captured and
congealed by the powers of evil, an incident parallel to the
Son's silencing of the Deep. As Sin and Death launch into
Chaos, Milton uses a geographical figure:

> As when two Polar Winds blowing adverse
> Upon the *Cronian* Sea, together drive
> Mountains of Ice, that stop th' imagin'd way
> Beyond *Petsora* Eastward, to the rich
> *Cathaian* Coast. (x.289–93)

The scene is repeated in miniature on earth:

> *Boreas* and *Caecias* and *Argestes* loud
> And *Thrascias* rend the Woods and Seas upturn;
> With adverse blast up-turns them from the South
> *Notus* . . . (x.699–702)

Thus the image of the salt, bare island in Book XI ties the
final knot in a thread which has been involved in some of the
high points of the poem. Its effectiveness in itself is great;
but much greater when we remember that the first uptorn
mountain was Satan himself; and that these images of disaster still form part of our own disordered world, with an
ultimate analogue in Hell. This series also serves to underline the integral quality of Milton's poem; his instances are
"real," a part of mythical history; at the same time they are

great symbols of the ideal forces behind the war of worlds. And the passage in Book XI is not exhausted even by the weight of exegesis in the preceding pages, which has not done justice to the proliferation of meanings that can be related to it. Like most of Milton's images, it is complex by virtue not of ambiguity but of fecundity of reference, a power of drawing into itself other events of the mythical cycle. It is, obviously, a nexus for Milton's sea imagery, persistent through the early books of the epic, and harking back to *Lycidas.* The ocean for him is usually destructive, but sometimes beneficently so, the main example being the Deluge itself. So, drowned Paradise is succeeded by "a Paradise within thee, happier far." The archetypal sea of *Paradise Lost,* Chaos, is described as "the Womb of Nature and perhaps her grave" (ii.911), conveying neatly the ambivalent connotations of womb and tomb that we have learned to read in water-imagery. Once more, remote places in the poem are given mythical affinity through allusion and image.

A severely structured universe is essential to Milton's mythical vision, where clear outlines and pure, complete beings are part of the landscape. The definite, morally significant "places" of *Paradise Lost,* the solidity of the poem's outlines in space, its intimations of mortality and history within those outlines, and the interlocked intricacy of its verbal and imagistic patterns, are part of a world-view that we can know only through the hearsay of myth. The world of *Paradise Lost,* when we first see it, is a complete world; it ends by being a ruined one. But before it can be broken, the great structure must be built. It must stand before us, solid, finished, composed of contending stresses in perfect balance; and in the gigantic pyramid of his poem, Milton has given us this distant world, held for an instant within the sweep of a single vision.

IV

THE LANGUAGE OF PARADISE LOST

The subject of Milton's diction is well-trodden though disputed territory, and there are many directions from which it can be approached. Only one direction will be followed here, and only those strands of the epic diction of the poem picked out, that seem directly related to the poem's mythic design. In every long poem, the poet is faced with the problem of reconciling variety of texture and continuity of effect; this difficulty, and the further one that the theme of a long poem (though not necessarily the treatment of the theme) precedes the actual composition in a way that it often does not in the composition of a lyric, means that the choice of "a diction," a language, assumes the status of a problem in itself, semi-detached from its real exercise in practice. The choice, for Milton, was partly determined, not only by the standard devices of epic, but by the desire to produce an epic "tone" more pervasive than any device could provide. The classical epics, and sixteenth-century Italian poetry, offered some suggestions; [1] in English, there was Spenser, and DuBartas in Sylvester's version. Other demands, more important though more subtle, made by the myth itself, manifested themselves in still other ways in the linguistic fabric of *Paradise Lost,* and with these we shall be mainly concerned.

A statistical starting-point may be useful: the comparatively small number of different words used in *Paradise Lost,* relative to its great length and complexity.[2] We have already seen that Milton's effects depend partly on repetition and variation, which at once cut down on the breadth of his vocabulary, since the structurally repetitive form of a mythological poem must be carried, in part, by a system of verbal reminiscence. And, as an epic poet, he was doubly limited, being bound not only by the generally narrowing influence of every convention, but by a particular rule that prescribed the use of a set diction. Thus epic practice and the nature of his subject cooperated to reduce his vocabulary. The subject, of course, was fundamentally conservative as well as mythical; the fable of *Paradise Lost* was probably the most familiar of all stories to Milton's readers, as Homer's had been for his audience. Furthermore, it was a religious story, authoritatively presented in a sacred book. Milton could not tell his tale exactly as he chose, and in many cases even thought himself well-advised to follow closely the wording of the Bible.

An epic theme was traditionally "single," even though it was episodically varied; it excluded much in the interests of unity, and exclusiveness of theme, too, played its part in reducing or distilling Milton's diction. He wrote that "the epic poet, who adheres at all to the rule of that species of composi-

[1] F. T. Prince has written well on this "influence" in *The Italian Element in Milton's Verse* (Oxford, 1954).
[2] Eight thousand words, as against 12,000 for Shakespeare. Otto Jespersen, *Language* (New York, 1923), p. 126.

tion, does not profess to describe the whole life of the hero whom he celebrates, but only some particular action of his life." [3] Elevation, not breadth, is the principal dimension of epic. Unity and elevation demand that there should be a single — even, in a sense, a simple — effect produced in the reader, and this end is not to be accomplished by a style with a verbally complex surface. These strictures apply with special urgency to Milton, whose epic portrays all history in a huge triptych. Its singleness is made up of terrible complexity, in much the same way that Michelangelo's Miltonic *Last Judgment* in the Sistine Chapel forces unity to emerge from a mass of violently moving figures. Milton follows his own rule in treating a "particular action" of Adam's life; but it is an action toward which all the mythical events point, and from which all human history flows. His themes are given physical unity by means of a relatively simple, architecturally conceived structure; his diction works to support and clarify that structure, by emphasizing its keystones and cornerstones and points of stress. It also provides the massive effects of surface that are necessary to make texture complement structure in mapping the significant areas of the mythical universe.

Simplicity was the keynote not only of the epic theme, but of the personages as well, whose "greatness" was considered, by the Renaissance at any rate, to be exemplary and "universal." Spenser had praised "Homere, who in the persons of Agamemnon and Ulysses hath ensampled a good governour and a vertuous man." [4] The epic poet must maintain "the grandeur of generality," even while recounting the story of a particular hero. The epic hero, though not "unreal," was traditionally remote in one way or another; and characteri-

---

[3] *Second Defense of the People of England, SM,* p. 1157.

[4] Letter to Ralegh, *Poetical Works,* ed. R. E. Neil Dodge (Boston, 1936), p. 136.

zation at these upper levels of generality is, relatively speaking, a simple affair. As the poet approaches more closely the uniqueness of individuality, distinctions proliferate, and he is driven to rifle the language in order to capture them precisely. The force that compelled the gnarled, nervous diction of Gerard Manley Hopkins was this very urge to render "inscapes" exactly; and precision of detail, with its corresponding virtues of freshness and resourcefulness in diction, has remained our criterion for poetry — it is what modern readers are trained to look for because, like Hopkins, they value the "precious object." [5] What they are not trained to see is the kind of universality contained in the formulas of epic diction, the recurrent epithets that express the human awareness of permanence. The epic world is larger than life-size, its patterns conformed to that part of us that belongs to our species rather than to a particular time, place, and parentage.

The demand for detailed visual impressions in poetry is an illegitimately limiting one, born of a distrust in the mind's constructions, and going back ultimately to an exaggerated humility before the glories of nature. One of its symptoms is the failure of language, ending logically in the doctrine that reality must be shown, not spoken.[6] Modern criticism, if not modern poetry, is still too often chained to T. E. Hulme's proposition that "the great aim is accurate, precise, and definite description." Hulme himself interpreted this statement narrowly and defined poetry as "a visual concrete"

[5] Hopkins himself identified inscape with "distinctiveness," contrasting it with the "more balanced and Miltonic style" which he hoped to achieve "in time." *Poems of Gerard Manley Hopkins,* ed. W. H. Gardner (3rd ed., London, 1956), p. 205.

[6] Cf. Bertrand Russell's Introduction to Ludwig Wittgenstein, *Tractatus Logico-Philosophicus* (London, 1922), pp. 8–11: "That which has to be in common between the sentence and the fact cannot, so he contends, be itself in turn *said* in language. It can . . . only be *shown.* . . . It results from this view that nothing correct can be said in philosophy."

art, making the reader "continuously see a physical thing." [7]
Milton's verse is primarily polemical and normative in style
(though not in strategy); nevertheless, these criteria might
be stretched to fit it, if our ideas of "seeing" had not
dwindled to admit only what is reflected on the retina, and
our ideas of "a physical thing" not been reduced to the
product of external sense impressions. T. S. Eliot's notorious
opinion that "Milton may be said never to have seen anything" [8] is intelligible only in the light of this background,
whereby visual detail illicitly became the standard of valid
imagery. Milton's images and words are counters in a good
sense; to paraphrase Eliot, they are objects that become the
formula for a general emotion or attitude — the attitude
always appropriate to a certain situation, regardless of what
supplementary emotions may be appropriate to the accidents
of its manifestations. The formula and its "significance" are,
in myth, of course inseparable.

A parallel confusion about Milton's diction emerges from
the argument that exalts the "musical" or "vague" qualities
of his verse to compensate for a supposed failure in accuracy
of vision and expression. It is based on the belief that the
general is equivalent to the indistinct, a romantic confusion
between "sublimity" and vagueness. This muddle, which has
a distinguished ancestry, was perpetuated unintentionally in
Macaulay's contrast between "the exact details of Dante"
and "the dim intimations of Milton." The intention of his
essay, however, was not to stress Milton's "dimness" but to
capture the suggestiveness of his images. The verse of *Paradise Lost* can validly be called suggestive because it must
allow private manifestations of the archetypes to form in the
mind of every reader. It appeals to individual human imag-

---

[7] *Speculations,* ed. Herbert Read (New York, 1924), pp. 132–34.
[8] "A Note on the Verse of John Milton," *ESEA,* XX (1936), 37.

inations to reconstruct meanings that are not individual. Macaulay's description of the effect produced by Milton's poetry finely conveys the reverberatory quality of mythical verse. "No sooner are [his words] pronounced, than the past is present and the distant near. New forms of beauty start at once into existence, and all the burial-places of the memory give up their dead." [9]

The outlines of Milton's persons and places, though they are not particularized by many details, are perfectly clear, the subject being a world of essences. They are not, certainly, clear when obscurity is part of their substance; some of the landscapes of Hell and Chaos, or the dazzling visions of God, "dark with excessive bright," are shown with necessarily blurred edges. But in general, because the subject is mythical, the objects are large and definite, grand with the grandeur of epic generality, but not *vague*. One need not suppose that the Ideas were vague to Plato, nor that Milton saw his figures indistinctly because he saw them on an heroic scale. The classicism of the Renaissance produced effects similar to Milton's in other arts — for example, in the figures of Michelangelo. "For him, the human race was not the humanity of this world, with its thousands of different individuals, but a race apart, transposed into the colossal." [10] A like clarity and simplicity of form appears in the plastic figures of *Paradise Lost*.

> Two of far nobler shape erect and tall,
> Godlike erect, with native Honour clad
> In naked Majestie seemd Lords of all,
> And worthie seemd, for in thir looks Divine

[9] "Milton" (1825), *Miscellaneous Works,* ed. Lady Trevelyan (5 vols., New York, n.d.), I, 28, 22.

[10] Heinrich Wölfflin, *Classic Art,* trans. Peter and Linda Murray (London 1952), p. 39.

> The image of thir glorious Maker shon,
> Truth, Wisdome, Sanctitude severe and pure, . . .
> For contemplation hee and valour formd,
> For softness shee and sweet attractive Grace. (iv.288–98)

Both poet and painter were striving to combine physical and abstract qualities into single, luminous shapes, though the means adopted necessarily differ. Milton in the opening words, *erect, tall, godlike,* is giving a notation for a perfect *human* figure, as distinct from "all kind Of living Creatures" which Satan has already seen. He refers, therefore, to the distinctively human upright stance, and in *godlike* to innumerable remembered versions of "the gods," chiefly classical, present in his readers' imaginations from their experience of tradition, that is, art and poetry. Around these generalized traditional images are grouped the "abstractions" summed up in them: majesty, truth, and so on. This habit of naming qualities and attaching them to the central figures is persistent in *Paradise Lost,* and it is not casual or careless. It is connected with Milton's feeling for the incarnate substantiality of "qualities" in the world he was depicting — a feeling whose results are everywhere apparent in phrases like "naked Majestie" or "that first naked Glorie" (ix.1115). Because the glory of Adam and Eve was luminous and immanent, the description is as apt as "glorious nakedness" would be, indeed, more apt, for their glory was a central fact which their nakedness merely served. It is not enough to dismiss such phrases as latinisms; more than one function is performed by poetic language.

Many influences, therefore — the formulas of epic diction, the limitations of the "single subject," the ontological peculiarities of the events and persons — came together to help form the style of *Paradise Lost.* It is a style alien to us, partly because of our reading habits, and the assumptions about reality that lie beneath them, and also because we cannot regard the motives behind the myth's reconstruction as valid. Their validity for Milton is attested by the vigor of his efforts to adapt old moulds to his "unattempted" matter. Epic characteristics were combined by him in a new way to fit his purposes, and broadened by the addition of new functions. One new, or extended, function, has been examined in the third chapter: the use of repeated words as a mnemonic aid and, in consequence, a structural principle. There, however, the stable rather than the dynamic aspect of the theme was stressed. The other major part of Milton's structure is the violent movement that, against a background of Hell, Heaven, and Earth, expresses the moral meaning of the poem. The war between good and evil was a part of Milton's myth; so, although there is motion upward and downward, there is also balance and tension between the opposites and the actors that embody them, a tension expressed primarily through language.

The world of myth is a dramatic world — a world of actions, of forces, of conflicting powers. In every phenomenon of nature it sees the collision of these powers. Mythical perception is always impregnated with these emotional qualities. Whatever is seen or felt is surrounded by a special atmosphere — an atmosphere of joy or grief, of anguish, of excitement, of exultation or depression. Here we cannot speak of "things" as dead of indifferent stuff. All objects are benignant or malignant, friendly or inimical, familiar or uncanny, alluring and fascinating or repellent and threatening.[11]

Milton's poetic world is inhabited by these potent "things," alluring or threatening, and their gigantic collisions are visible on every level. Milton's awareness of the contrarieties of life was profound; it was expressed in a war

[11] Cassirer, *Essay on Man,* pp. 76–77.

and balance of imagery from his earliest writings. "It is well known that light and darkness have been divided from one another by an implacable hatred from the very beginning of time," he wrote in one of the Academic Exercises;[12] and in *Paradise Lost* the warriors of light and darkness enact their divisions on a cosmic stage. The War in Heaven is an ancient mythical motif; it follows naturally on the Creation myth where unity becomes multiplicity and antagonism is made possible. The division of the One into the Many, an improvement on the vast confusion of formless being, nevertheless sharpens the awareness of opposites, by disentangling them and aligning them in distinct camps that soon acquire a moral significance. War in Heaven is the result. At the same time, harmony is made possible by this separation, and the imagery of music and rhythmical organic life counterbalances warfare in Milton's poetry. St. Augustine had written:

As these contraries opposed do give the saying [in rhetoric] an excellent grace, so is the world's beauty composed of contrarieties, not in figure but in nature. This is plain in Ecclesiasticus, in this verse: "Against evil is good, and against death is life; so is the godly against the sinner: so look for in all the works of the highest, two and two, one against one." [13]

A statement by Jung may be adduced as evidence for the survival-power of this idea:

I see in all happening the play of opposites, and derive from this conception my idea of psychic energy. I hold that psychic energy involves the play of opposites in much the same way as physical energy involves a difference of potential, which is to say, the existence of such opposites as warm and cold, high and low.[14]

12 *Private Correspondence*, p. 58.
13 *City of God*, Book XI, ch. 18. I, 327.
14 *Modern Man in Search of a Soul*, trans. W. S. Dell and C. E. Baynes (New York, 1933), p. 138.

Exactly "such opposites" and many others are visible in
Paradise Lost from the moment when Milton, soaring above
the Aonian Mount, views the deep tract of Hell; and the
"play of opposites" — "not in figure, but in nature" — is
the governing principle in his verbal reconstruction of the
Garden.

Strenuous contest permeates the poem: its meaning and
all aspects of the techniques that enforce the meaning. The
poem is about the most crucial change in history, and the
struggle that brought it about; as Milton had written, "If
we look but on the nature of elemental and mixed things, we
know they cannot suffer any change of one kind or quality
into another, without the struggle of contrarieties." [15] His
vocabulary embodies this struggle on the fundamental plane
of connotative language. Unlike Homer, whose epithets are
almost invariably attached to one object or personage, Milton uses for each major "idea" made incarnate in the poem a
fluid stock of modifiers, all tending in a similar direction,
within which he can choose freely. The result is repetition,
not of identical epithets, but of *groups* of words whose connotations support each other, and contrast with other groups
that modify opposing concepts. Milton makes his words take
sides; the objects of the poem, both animate and inanimate,
along with their names, are aligned in opposing ranks and
forced to participate in the War in Heaven that is being continued on earth.

Josephine Miles, in her statistical study of poetic vocabu-
laries, has found Milton's six favorite adjectives to be: *good,
high, fair, bad, happy,* and *sweet.*[16] Statistical methods, whatever their merit or demerit in the study of other poets, have
some validity when applied to a writer who made deliberate

[15] *Reason of Church Government, SM,* p. 520.
[16] *Major Adjectives in English Poetry* (Berkeley, 1946), p. 308.

use of repetition for a multitude of purposes. All the words Miss Miles picks out are, significantly, normative in connotation. *High, fair,* and *sweet* belong to a much-used category of Miltonic words expressing a sensory and a moral or "spiritual" fact simultaneously. Among his favorite terms, other than adjectives, Miss Miles lists *heaven, God, man, earth, live, death.* Already, in this handful of words, we catch a glimpse of the antagonists of *Paradise Lost:* good and bad, God and man, heaven and earth, life and death.[17] Miss Miles' analysis bears out statistically the impression we get from reading Milton's poem — that his vocabulary is chosen with some other end in mind than pictorial exactness. The words are there because of their emotional, value-conferring weight, and though not usually exhaustively descriptive of external attributes, they do succeed in suggesting the *attitude* that Milton wishes us to take up, that is, the qualities of objects to which we are supposed to react morally. Not admiration but partisanship is demanded, and it can be instilled only by verbal emphasis. The vocabulary is put to work establishing standards, even though it may not increase our knowledge or complete our mental picture of the object. Not even small words are allowed to be neutral; there is a persistent contrast between words like *up* and *down, above* and *below.*

The phalanxes of terms marshalled by Milton on each side of his battle-line distill the essential qualities of the contestants. On one hand: dark, foul, horrid, fiery, sad, gloomy, forlorn, wild, dreadful, cold, burnt, dire, deep, grim, hopeless; on the other: glorious, bright, happy, high, fair, warm, vital, golden, sweet, melodious, clear. In Paradise, a third list can be gathered: soft, gentle, fresh, pure, tender, cool, kindly,

17 It is likely that *Hell* would have to be included in this list of most-favored words, if one counted the unusually large number of synonyms for it in *Paradise Lost: pit, gulf, deep,* and so on. Heaven and Earth are generally called by their own names.

delicious, mild, profuse. To set together in this way the modifiers of Milton's basic "places" is to see more clearly how his method may be called centripetal. None of these adjectives contains even a submerged suggestion of metaphor, as it is used in *Paradise Lost;* they encourage, rather, a reconstruction by the reader of objects that once contained a single luminous quality (or an opaque one), since shattered into many colors and variously named, because our imperfect vision cannot bear total light or total darkness. No single word can summarize Hell for us; it is only by joining qualities that the poet can approximate the texture of his archetypes. To join other *objects,* as in metaphor, is only confusing. Not analysis, but synthesis, a reabsorption into the original source, is wanted. Something of the intent and method behind this process is suggested in an important passage of Milton's prose, centered on a mythological metaphor.

Truth indeed came once into the world with her divine master, and was a perfect shape most glorious to look on: but when he ascended, and his apostles after him were laid asleep, then straight arose a wicked race of deceivers, who, as that story goes of the Egyptian Typhon with his conspirators, how they dealt with the good Osiris, took the virgin Truth, hewed her lovely form into a thousand pieces, and scattered them to the four winds. From that time ever since, the sad friends of Truth, such as durst appear, imitating the careful search that Isis made for the mangled body of Osiris, went up and down gathering up limb by limb still as they could find them. We have not yet found them all, . . . nor ever shall do, till her Master's second coming.[18]

A technique of moral description that strove to reassemble the "lovely form" of Truth can be observed in almost any group of lines: the first glance at Adam and Eve, or this sight of Chaos:

18 *Areopagitica, SM,* pp. 747–48.

> On heav'nly ground they stood, and from the shore
> They view'd the vast, immeasurable Abyss
> Outrageous as a Sea, dark, wasteful, wilde . . . (vii.210–12)

Of the seven adjectives, not one is neutral, except perhaps *vast,* which in the context of the poem has a negative charge since it is ordinarily applied, as here, to Chaos. *Heav'nly* stations Christ and the angels with Milton's habitual definiteness in the geography of his universe. Its emotional meaning is expanded in the metaphor (though it is more than that) of the safe shore and the dangerous ocean. *Immeasurable,* though a literal description of Chaos, also has emotive overtones: extravagance, being beyond or outside all rule or measure, in defiance of order. These connotations are reinforced by the anger of *outrageous* and the uncontrollability of *wild.* It is interesting to compare with this passage the lines spoken by God of himself on the preceding page, where he is saying some of the same things that Milton says about Chaos, but with a different implication.

> Boundless the Deep, because I am who fill
> Infinitude. (vii.168–69)

Boundless is rather different in its reverberations from *immeasurable;* it hints at *freedom* from limit and restraint rather than rebellion against reasonable measure. *Bound* is the word used by Raphael in his account of the scale of being in Book V: "bounds Proportiond to each kind" (478–79); and in a preceding line, the Son is to bid the Deep "within appointed bounds be Heav'n and Earth" (vii.167). *Boundless* is therefore appropriate for the Being at the head of the scale, the unlimited Creator of limited creatures.[19] The

---

[19] Milton uses *boundless* on two other occasions in the poem. In the first, it again modifies *deep,* and is again connected with the power of God; Satan con-

word *infinitude,* traditionally associated with divinity and properly awe-inspiring to the century that had rediscovered it, supports these associations. *Fill* (set deliberately at a noticeable point in the line) aligns the plenitude of God against the emptiness of opposing forces: Chaos earlier is called "a vast vacuitie" (ii.932).

In two other adjectives for Chaos, *dark* and *wasteful,* Milton brings together two persistent threads of imagery: the dark/light antithesis that for him, as for Spenser and Shakespeare, embodied profound intuitions of value; and the theme of fertility vs. barrenness. *Wasteful* encompasses both the waste land and the "waste fertility" of *Comus* which chokes itself and brings death at the other extreme. It is an epithet peculiarly suited to Chaos, at once an inferno of fruitlessly warring elements, and the source of all fertility, when God commands. Finally, Milton's passage as a whole contains the ghosts of past descriptions and the shadows of those to come, the most important being Satan on the brink of Hell, about to plunge into the "wilde Abyss" (ii.917 ff.), the pavilion of Chaos spread "wide on the wasteful Deep" (ii.961), and the expedition of Sin and Death into "the waste Wide Anarchie of *Chaos* damp and dark" (x.282–83). The word *wasteful* (or *waste*) in particular resounds through the poem, always introducing a note at once of anarchy and of barrenness. In another instance it also connotes a deathly

---

jectures that God's thunder has ceased "to bellow through the vast and boundless Deep" in pursuit of the fallen angels (i.177). The emphasis is on the immensity of the gulf, a function of the divine vengeance. In Book III, the word is used with a more specific connotation. Satan has alighted on the shell of the world, which to him "now seems a boundless Continent Dark, waste, and wild" (iii.423–24). *Seems* is important here, since Milton has just carefully defined the bounds and purpose of earth's "first convex" (418 ff.), and noted that from a distance it looks like what it is, a globe. To Satan, a mere speck on the surface, however, it appears vast and threatening — hence *boundless*.

tedium — as in wasting time or wasting away: Satan and his angels are "condemn'd To waste Eternal dayes in woe and pain" (ii.694–95). Later, man's sin has "let in these wasteful Furies," Sin and Death, who will "waste and havoc" the world (x.617, 620). The ramifications of this term provide a good example of "typical" Miltonic usage because, though *wasteful* is used in almost all the senses we normally assign to it, and is even stretched and doubled if necessary, the effect is to add resonance rather than true ambiguity. The connotations all point in the same direction, toward destruction and dreariness, and Milton's habit on the whole was to choose words whose variant meanings would reinforce rather than balance or contrast with each other; contrast came between words, not within them. Other instances can be found among the latinate words that are to be understood in both the root and the derived sense, like the one describing the angel Abdiel: *fervent,* at once burning "in a flame of zeale," and eager.

The adoption of a vocabulary internally cooperative rather than rebellious serves a basic simplicity of vision that was to be projected through language. If Milton was to present the objects of the poem as the archetypes of certain virtues and vices, clarity and consistency were the most important requirements for his diction. In the world of *Paradise Lost,* the great opposites exist as yet unconfused; "the terrible ambiguity of immediate experience" has not yet bewildered human understanding, and the realities of life lie simple, sensuous, and passionate before the naked eye. It is not only that Milton, in describing Paradise, had to give us an image of something at once too intimate and too universal to be precisely drawn. It is also that the "something" was of a different quality from the objects ordinarily depicted in poetry. Milton has been accused of oversimplifying;

but the essence of his subject was, literally, simplicity —
though he also shows the murderous birth of archetypal
dualism. Thus, his characteristic verbal (as distinct from
syntactical) idiom is direct; he speaks of important simple
objects, narrowed and defined by simple adjectives which
characterize rather than attempt to describe exhaustively.
And characterization is usually related to the basic moral
structure of the poem. "Harmonious sound," "furious
winds," "warm prolific humour," "copious Fruit," "liquid,
pure, transparent, Elemental Air" — these examples culled
at random from the account of Creation represent Milton's
normal practice; they are not, of course, inaccurate visually
or physically, but their most important area of accuracy is
emotive or moral.

This is not the place to discuss so-called "poetic diction"
or Milton's responsibility for it, except in a negative way.
Insofar as poetic diction is periphrastic, on the model of
"fleecy care" and "finny tribe," it is not typically Miltonic,
though one can find instances enough in the wide fabric of
Paradise Lost. Noticeable and awkward periphrasis gathers
chiefly when Milton is attempting to describe a dull technical process in the grand manner: the invention of cannon
in Book VI, Eve's culinary arts, or Adam's musing on fire-
building in Book X. These subjects are extraneous to the
main themes and out of key with the rest of the poem because they are ethically neutral, that is, scientific. Milton's
efforts in these places usually produce a devilish glut of
latinate words: "concocted and adusted," "incentive reed,"
"with matter sere foment." The *effects* of the cannon have a
moral significance, however, and with them Milton resumes
his major subject and a congenial style. When the guns are
fired, he uses one of his persistent images, which is also an
idea: the violation of the physical body of nature; the shot,

> Emboweld with outragious noise the Air,
> And all her entrails tore, disgorging foule
> Thir devillish glut. (vi.587–89)

Outragious, foule, and *devillish* are all consonant with the poem's moral scheme, in which Satan's engines are duly located.

The conditions of the poem obviously excluded certain poetic devices and styles from *Paradise Lost*. Milton's language is not, like Donne's, "a recreation of thought into feeling," nor is it the vehicle of an inverted process, also found in Donne, which translates feeling into the modes of discursive logic. Nor could Milton make use, in any extensive way, of multi-leveled Shakespearean language. The typical unit of the Miltonic style cannot be the dramatic image, standing for something else — explicit in allegory, implicit in "oblique" poetry — nor the statement drawing symbolic implication from a concrete presentation, as Wordsworth's verse often does. All these styles, to put the point spectacularly, are styles for a fallen world. All of them are varieties of metaphor, describing an object by comparing it with something else, joining two universes of discourse. Metaphor is a device of rhetoric and dialectic, important ways of explaining and knowing for us, who are obliged to analyze before we can understand. But dialectic itself was one of the unhappy results of the Fall; it is the fallen angels who debate. When the object is completely seen at once, metaphor is unnecessary; it is saturated with the "meaning" that we usually apply to it from outside.

Stylistically, Milton's vision of a single interconnected universe meant that, even when he used metaphor and simile, the vehicle could almost without warning shift and become the tenor. A signal example comes in Book V of *Paradise*

Lost, when Raphael is describing to Adam the great chain of being. Objects close to God are

> more refin'd, more spiritous, and pure,
> As neerer to him plac't or neerer tending
> Each in thir several active Spheares assignd,
> Till body up to spirit work, in bounds
> Proportiond to each kind. So from the root
> Springs lighter the green stalk, from thence the leaves
> More aerie, last the bright consummate floure
> Spirits odorous breathes: flours and thir fruit
> Mans nourishment, by gradual scale sublim'd
> To vital Spirits aspire, to animal,
> To intellectual. (v.475–85)

The image of the plant with its bright consummate flower is at once a stage in the argument and an epitome of the whole subject. This delicate modulation from the main subject to the image, and back again to the tenor, is carried partly by the play on *spirits,* a favorite type of word with Milton, combining a physical with a metaphysical meaning. The passage is also a good example of the way in which subject and technique unite in the poem. This close-knit world is like a universe of mirrors where it is as impossible to tell what is reflection and what is "real," as to tell when the poet is using figurative language, and when literal. Only the source of light is constant. Finally, Raphael in choosing the plant image is of course illustrating the microcosm/macrocosm relationship where the structures of all beings find counterparts in others.

The typical unit of the Miltonic style is the direct adjectival phrase, like "bright consummate flour," summing up qualities (nearness to the light, supremacy, fulfilment), rather than reaching out, by means of metaphor, to link objects into the chain of relationships we have imposed on the world. The persistence of normative epithets (both *bright* and *consummate* are value-words in Milton's world) follows naturally from the kind of poem *Paradise Lost* is. It is not a philosophical poem in the manner of the *Essay on Man* or *The Prelude,* or even *Paradise Regained.* Although it contains plenty of arguments, it is not itself an argument, but a presentation, and the images represented are not illustrations but causes of moral events. Moral efficacy must therefore be manifest in them and shown to be part of the poem's meaning; but this cannot be done by discoursing on moral problems. Johnson observed, with some regret, that "splendid passages containing lessons of morality or precepts of prudence occur seldom." [20] There is no place in *Paradise Lost* for the grave classical splendors of Ben Jonson's great odes, "the Stand" upon moral precept: "It is not growing like a tree . . . " Still less can Milton allow himself the admonitory gestures to the reader with which Sylvester's Du-Bartas bristles: "Thou scoffing Atheist . . ." "Know (bold Blasphemer) . . .", "Yet think not . . ." The dramatic, undidactic quality of Milton's epic emerges clearly against the background of the *Divine Weekes,* where divergent intent and execution transform a "similar" subject from myth into a quaint scientific and historical chronicle. For Milton, the myth and its meaning were not to be distinguished; so we find him, most of the time, describing something actually going on or existing — characters acting and speaking, Paradise or Hell in their substantial reality. Overt "author's comment" is confined to a few set pieces like the lines on wedded love. The burden of implied meaning is therefore shifted partly onto the language itself, in particular the modifiers. This process, indeed, goes on in all poetry; it is

[20] *Lives of the Poets,* I, 176.

especially vital in *Paradise Lost* because the implications are weightier and the percentage of explicit comment is less than we are prepared to allow in a poem of such length.

Milton's phrases normally join a spiritual or moral theme (through the modifier) to its embodiment or "subject" (the noun); though "join" is misleading: the adjective reminds us of qualities inherent in the object, to which we have given abstract names. There is a limited analogy in the epithets of classical epic. Every reader remembers that Aeneas' distinctive quality is to be *pius* and so, too, we recall as single units rather than separate concepts "Achilles of the swift feet," "Zeus the cloud-gatherer," "horse-pasturing Argos" in the *Iliad*. "Names, or nouns, carry with them descriptive terms, of varying appropriateness, which adhere so closely that they are scarcely more than extensions of the noun." [21] In Milton's hands, the appropriateness became invariably exact, and the noun-adjective relation was given, so to speak, a metaphysical sanction in the unique status of the paradisal world.

Milton often chose the simple relations analyzed in Aristotle's categories to distinguish his nouns. When Uriel points out to Satan the moon, "that opposite fair Star" (iii.727), one adjective simply indicates position; the other, *fair*, is again a word of physical-*cum*-spiritual significance. A number of "pointing" words like *opposite* turn up because direction is essential to the structure of *Paradise Lost*. But the majority of Milton's epithets, like *fair*, combine with some straightforward quality an additional weight of thematic implication. In reading the poem, one is scarcely conscious of the difference between these descriptive words that mediate between two planes of being, and adjectives that would ordinarily not be considered concrete, but here have a kind of

[21] Lattimore, Introduction to *The Iliad*, p. 39.

physical margin. "Emotive" non-physical terms in the context of Milton's larger intention are felt to be as "concrete" as sensory words like *bright, soft, sweet,* or *black.* We become used to noticing two aspects of an adjective at once, and so we add a certain depth or heaviness to terms like *fierce, blessed, grim, faithful, harmless,* or *violent.* Some examples in phrases depict the threatening or friendly landscapes of myth: "baleful streams," "grateful Twilight," "dismal Gates"; or give definite resonance to a neutral word: "innumerable sound," "sad exclusion." Or, as emotions receive a body when they are enacted by the characters, adjectives acquire solidity with adverbial force: "gestures fierce," "yet faithful how they stood." Almost all of Milton's epithets are used, in one way or another, to fit the noun into the scheme of the whole poem, and so they tend to accumulate still more meaning as it goes along.

The adjective-noun pattern may give way to two adjectives, or two nouns; but the intention is the same: to show simultaneously more than one aspect of every object, personage, or event, the percept and the concept at once. For this, Milton often uses matching phrases or double adjectives that interact with each other to produce the two dimensions, abstract/concrete.

> Wingd with red Lightning and impetuous rage. (i.175)

> The seat of desolation, voyd of light,
> Save what the glimmering of these livid flames
> Casts pale and dreadful. (i.181–83)

> Gay Religions full of Pomp and Gold. (i.372)

Contrast is Milton's most persistent method of bringing home to his reader the nature of the antagonistic qualities inhabiting the epic world. As he wrote elsewhere, "No man

apprehends what vice is so well as he who is truly virtuous,
no man knows Hell like him who converses most in
Heaven." [22] Effects are heightened, or deepened, by being
set off against each other; this is not a process of metaphor,
not comparison, but direct antithesis. The "cumbrous Elements" at the Creation (iii.715) take on full value only in the
next line, when they are implicitly contrasted with "this
Ethereal quintessence of Heav'n." In a casual allusion in the
opening book, Milton reminds us of the angels' lost realm
by linking it with its opposite, as he records Satan's first
venture into his kingdom:

> Uneasie steps
> Over the burning Marle, not like those steps
> On Heavens Azure. (i.295-97)

The involutions of the myth, from bright Heaven to burning
Hell, can thus be traced through the poem's very texture.
The predicament of the fallen angels requires that their
former and their present condition both be kept constantly
in view. So Milton writes of them (in the simile of the
forest) as a "stately growth though bare" (i.614); the first
and last words are joined respectively to Heaven and to
Hell. For contrast between. rather than within his characters,
he may link them in a phrase with one or another of the
main antitheses: Uriel, "the sharpest sighted Spirit of all
in Heav'n" (iii.691); "*Mammon, the least erected Spirit that
fell*" (i.679).

An epithet several times used for Earth — "this frail
World" — shows the combination in a single phrase of a dual
connotation. The world is physically frail, its crystal shell
subject to the invasions of Satan, Sin and Death; and the men

[22] *Doctrine and Discipline, SM*, p. 616.

who will live there are prey to the moral weakness that we sum up in the expression "human frailty." The same sort of effect is visible in Milton's habitual use of *deep,* one of his key words. It is ambidextrous, both a noun and an adjective, and carries a trace of its other function when it is used as either. Concreteness and abstraction are consistently present in it. Thus, when we read of Satan "rackt with deep despare" (i.126), we remember that it is because he is in the "hollow Deep of Hell" (i.314); and the phrase "so deep a malice" (ii.382) takes on an added horror when we realize from what depth it has come. *High,* too, has twin meanings, as when Milton indicates the direction of Satan's fate in the lines —

> And som are fall'n, to disobedience fall'n,
> And so from Heav'n to deepest Hell; O fall
> From what high state of bliss into what woe! (v.541–43)

All the examples of the last few paragraphs have suggested how Milton's language becomes a vehicle for his themes. When he turns to pure description, where a weight of ethical or metaphysical meaning is not suitable, he follows the necessities of his subject, instead of creating them. In Book VII, the record of the Creation, the familiar creatures of earth appear in well-known dress; they are characterized by the realm they live in (water, shore, trees), or by simple physical attributes, or some traditional quality — as, "the prudent Crane." Here are the fish, "thir wav'd coats dropt with Gold," the swan with "Oarie feet," the "solemn Nightingal," "lion with Brinded main," the hippopotamus "ambiguous between Sea and Land," and a host of insects, "with spots of Gold and Purple, azure and green," like small unmalignant jewels. These descriptions are all so uncomplex and direct, so "general" even while remaining concrete, that we tend to slide over them and to suppose that Milton was carelessly performing a task to which his powers were not suited. But these birds and beasts do not inhabit a particular acre in England, nor are they seen by a single human being at a moment of time, like Hopkins' windhover. *Paradise Lost* cannot accommodate the herbals and bestiaries of DuBartas; its creatures are the ancestors of all later fauna, and must be made large enough to circumscribe their innumerable offspring. St. Bonaventura wrote, "In Paradise is no plantation save of eternal causes." [23] The inhabitants of Milton's Eden are the formal causes of the creatures we know, straight from the hand of "the sovran Planter" (iv.691), and can be represented only in their most essential features.

Milton's historical sense of the poetic and legendary tradition behind him made possible this kind of generalized imagery, and produced some of the characteristic effects of his style. An enormous weight of experience, vicarious and "racial" as well as personal, lends authority to the images of *Paradise Lost,* doing duty for the innocent but "unified" vision of our ancestors. Here are a few lines on the mount of Paradise.

> And higher then that Wall a circling row
> Of goodliest Trees loaden with fairest Fruit,
> Blossoms and Fruits at once of golden hue
> Appeerd, with gay enameld colours mixt:
> On which the Sun more glad impress'd his beams
> Then in fair Evening Cloud, or humid Bow,
> When God hath showrd the earth. (iv.146–52)

Underneath the phrase "goodliest Trees" is a feeling about what being a tree involves, and has always involved. Every tree is individual, but to the eye of the traditionalist it

---

[23] *Illuminationes in Hexaëmeron,* quoted in Wallerstein, *Studies in Seventeenth Century Poetic,* p. 204.

gathers to itself the feelings evoked and beauties possessed by all other trees as well. References to Hesperian fables and ambrosial fruit are quite natural here; they invoke important trees of the past, and notions that poets had about them. Milton's images often record in this way not one experience, but a composite of many experiences. Simple visual facts are used to summarize or represent the realities of remote times and places to which they are akin. The goodliest trees and fairest fruits of Paradise are invested with the associations surrounding their descendants in the world of time; Milton reconstructs the "eternal causes" from his knowledge of the generations that have passed since they were first planted in Paradise.

A similar expectation that a reader will be able to follow a gradual construction not only outside, but within the poem, underlies Milton's characterization of the major *personae* in *Paradise Lost*. By degrees, we are introduced to a many-sided but "single" entity, each epithet adding some essential attribute. Take *Abyss*, one of the names for Chaos, a key figure in the drama. It is called, first, *vast;* then "the dark unbottom'd infinite Abyss" (ii.405); later, *hollow, wild, nethermost, dark, desolate, immeasurable, vexed, untractable,* and "wide interrupt" (iii.83). From these terms, we can put together a gloss that will summarize what Milton wished us to know about the archetypal abyss. It is the negative counterpart, or perhaps the negative aspect, of God — an infinity living in the "nethermost" regions farthest removed from Heaven; in its deepest depth is Hell. It is Heaven's opposite, in being a waste land (*desolate*), subject to the passions of vexation, misrule, and rebellion (*untractable*); no light comes there. Its negativeness is defined by *hollow, unbottom'd,* and by *interrupt,* suggesting a vacancy in creation. But *vast* and *infinite* are still relevant, because the Abyss is potential divinity, the teeming source of worlds on which the Spirit of God has brooded. All this comes merely from the epithets used for *abyss* itself; our understanding is further expanded when we trace the image through its other names: *pit, gulf, deep.* Milton has thus substituted for a few adjectives of multiple meaning, an extensive technique of cumulative simple epithets, appropriate both to the "simple" mythic surface of the poem and its repetitive spatial structure.

A crucial variation on *abyss* comes in Book X, when fallen man exclaims:

> O Conscience, into what Abyss of fears
> And horrors hast thou driv'n me; out of which
> I find no way, from deep to deeper plung'd! (x.842–44)

It is a re-enactment of Satan's predicament: "my self am Hell" —

> And in the lowest deep a lower deep
> Still threatning to devour me opens wide. (iv.76–77)

Milton makes it clear that as Adam and Eve wander down into the lower world, they carry within them, like their descendant Sir Thomas Browne, all geography: Paradise, Chaos, and Hell. Henceforth the myth, which once occurred in fact, will be relived in a thousand shapes in man's soul, and will reappear in shadowy form in the productions of his mind. This transformation from the outer reality of myth to the inner reality of archetypal images was adumbrated also by St. Augustine: "If by 'abyss' we understand a great depth, is not man's heart an abyss? For what is there more profound than that abyss?" [24] Finally, at the very end, after

---

[24] *Enarrationes in Psalmos,* Psalm XLI, *An Augustine Synthesis,* ed. E. Przywara (New York, 1936), p. 421.

Adam has seen the drama of earthly existence, the Abyss re-appears as a living reality to swallow up what once emerged from it, and the wheel comes full circle after the fashion of all mythologies.

> How soon hath thy prediction, Seer blest,
> Measur'd this transient World, the Race of time,
> Till time stand fixt: beyond is all abyss,
> Eternitie, whose end no eye can reach. (xii.553–56)

Milton's treatment of his Abyss thus follows the threefold pattern of the myth in which it is an element. The archetype is established as a distinct unity; it is then broken and trans-ferred to the soul, where mythic warfare takes place "in the field of this world"; in the process, it is transmuted into a metaphor or allegorical image "standing for" an inner state: the "abyss of fears." Finally, when time stands fixed, there is a return to ultimate realities, "the literal and the metaphor-ical rushing together." [25]

In writing of his images, Milton faced a problem that confronts every mythologist: how to describe in verse, which must be concrete, an Idea at once unique and general. The problem had been solved (though it was not recognized in exactly these terms) by earlier epic poets and their classiciz-ing Renaissance followers, in a supernatural machinery of gods and goddesses, who by their action suggested the oper-ation of powerful "abstract" forces. Milton, whose poem consisted almost entirely of "supernatural machinery" meant to be taken literally, could not follow their precedent closely. But the ghosts of classical deities are in Milton's epithets that indicate power, worth, and place. The instances have been dissolved into their sources, the crooked images again made part of the one true history.

[25] C. S. Lewis, *Miracles* (New York, 1947), p. 192.

V

"INTO OUR FIRST WORLD":
MILTON'S IMAGERY

THE VISION OF HISTORY

The proposition that Milton's verse-texture is fundamentally unmetaphorical — far less figurative in *Paradise Lost,* indeed, than his ordinary prose style — will be quickly dismissed by those whose memory of the poem lives in such images as Satan's moonlike shield, or Eve the fairest unsupported flower. The epic simile, however, was traditionally a diversion, a little world in itself, which did not necessitate a change in the quality of the verse. The language within a long simile may remain, itself, unfigurative; in fact, the effect of closely-wrought metaphor may be confusing in such a context. Richmond Lattimore has reminded modern readers of the *Iliad* that "Homer does not use metaphor extensively," developing instead "the more explicit simile," in contrast to "the difficult austere figures of a Pindar or Sophocles." [1] Similarly, Milton abandoned the radically figurative style of his early poems — notably, *Lycidas* and certain passages of *Comus* — which critics like to call Shakespearean.

[1] Introduction to *The Iliad,* p. 41.

The author of *Paradise Lost* stands in relation to Shakespeare (and the young Milton) as Homer does to Sophocles in Mr. Lattimore's comparison. Both epic poets found it necessary to stop short of the complex metaphors that served the dramatists as instruments for psychological exploration and symbolic statement.

Homer's similes provide relief from the steady surge of heroic action, and widen the scope of his poems. Into the simile could be introduced familiar scenes to remind the listener of the world living on beyond the plains of Troy or Odysseus' storm-beaten vessel. On the whole, this precedent was followed, or at least honored, by epic poets up to Milton. In *Paradise Lost,* tradition is modified to weave the long similes more closely into the poem's structure and meaning. Milton's purpose was to absorb mythological themes into their myths, reassembling Truth as, in his figure, Isis reassembled the body of Osiris. His similes descend from the universals of myth to instances in history, legend, and nature, and so show something of the life-history of the archetypes. Thus Miltonic similes, like Miltonic diction, contribute to the tightly-knit pattern of the whole poem, and serve to underline the unities rather than the diversities of the mythological world.

Since history repeats, on a smaller scale, the grand outlines of pre-history, Milton allows his instances to become part of the fabric of *Paradise Lost* in their own right, not as mere metaphorical equivalents. Characteristic are these lines, as Satan approaches Heaven's gate:

> The Stairs were such as whereon *Jacob* saw
> Angels ascending and descending, bands
> Of Guardians bright, when he from *Esau* fled
> To *Padan-Aram* in the field of *Luz*,
> Dreaming by night under the open Skie,
> And waking cri'd, This is the Gate of Heav'n. (iii.510–15)

This passage begins as the vehicle of a greater tenor in the foreground; but it soon usurps the foreground itself and assumes its place in Milton's pattern as a relevant fragment of history. Most of the images in *Paradise Lost* thus have a substantial life of their own; they are "properties" rather than metaphors.[2]

The similes in *Paradise Lost* can be roughly divided into three groups according to subject, though the subjects often overlap or merge into one another. The most interesting, because most original, is the type which the general reader associates with Milton: the analogues from other mythologies, chiefly classical. They are central to his purpose of variety-in-unity, lending new dimensions to his basically simple themes; Milton was not merely indulging irresponsibly a "love of classical literature." The second and third types are those drawn from history, including the Bible, and those from nature. Analogies in the third group invoke particularly "elemental" nature: clouds, winds, volcanoes, lightning, sun spots, shooting stars, rainbows, mists.

The "classical" similes have been much discussed, their sources traced and their interpretations debated. Their pertinence to the major themes is clear enough in most cases; their usefulness as a descriptive technique, in a situation forbidding description, is to be noted. Three of the most famous groups of images will illustrate this: the comparison of Eden with pagan paradises, of the nuptial bower with the haunts of Pan, and of Eve with pagan goddesses. The first contains the celebrated reference to Ceres, with its submerged allusion to Eve in Proserpina, pointing forward both to the Ceres/Eve analogy (ix.395–96), and to the image of Eve as "fairest unsupported Flour" (ix.432). Both the Christian

---

[2] This distinction was made by Robert Bridges in his essay, "Poetic Diction," *Collected Essays, II & III* (London, 1928), p. 65 and *passim*. It has since become familiar.

and the Greek myth record the death of innocence at the hands of Hell's forces, a "separation by violence," as Bacon wrote, of the "ethereal spirit" from its native regions, to be "enclosed and imprisoned beneath the earth (which earth is represented by Pluto)." [3] The subterranean regions are almost always surrounded, in *Paradise Lost,* by suggestions of danger. Milton's technical purpose can be observed in the *form* of the simile as a whole. It is constructed on the plan of negative comparison that gave offense to Bentley, but reflects precisely the archetypal nature of the theme. "Not that fair field . . . not that sweet Grove . . . nor that *Nyseian* Ile . . . nor where *Abassin* Kings . . . " The structure is the same in the two other simile-groups: "*Pan* or *Silvanus* never slept" in a shadier bower; Eve outshines Diana: "*Delia's* self In gate surpass'd . . . more lovely fair Then Wood-Nymph." Just so, in another place, the Serpent is exalted above his offspring: "never since of Serpent kind Lovelier" (ix.504–5). Comparative adjectives are used throughout *Paradise Lost* when Milton is describing his major images; intensives are needed because the central objects themselves are superlative —

> *Adam* the goodliest man of men since borne
> His Sons, the fairest of her Daughters *Eve.* (iv.323–24)

No son or daughter can be quite as wonderful as these originals; in the same way no lesser garden or fair field "might with this Paradise Of Eden strive."

The result of assembling these varied instances is analogous to that produced by the modifiers surrounding Milton's important nouns: a broken image is reconstituted by fitting together the fragments that fallen man has been able to collect in his myths, and at the same time the status of the image as the original of and superior to all the fragments is

---

3 *De sapientia veterum, Works,* VI, 759.

established. An early essay at description by allusion can be found at the end of *Comus,* when the Spirit flies back to his haunt in "the broad fields of the sky." It is spoken of in terms of the classical paradises that appear in *Paradise Lost* as pale reflections of Eden: the Hesperides, Elysium where "eternal Summer dwels," the Garden of Adonis, the Bower of Cupid. Such descriptive/comparative functions are often joined, in the epic, to a prophetic use, as in the analogy between Eve and Pandora:

> in naked beauty more adorn'd,
> More lovely then *Pandora,* whom the Gods
> Endowd with all thir gifts, and O too like
> In sad event. (iv.713–16)

The comparative pattern is normal in the mythological allusions of *Paradise Lost;* it appears, too, in many of the historical references, for example, the description of Pandemonium, with its allusions to the wicked cities of men.

> Not *Babilon,*
> Nor great *Alcairo* such magnificence
> Equal'd in all thir glories, to inshrine
> *Belus* or *Serapis* thir Gods, or seat
> Thir Kings, when *Aegypt* with *Assyria* strove
> In wealth and luxurie. (i.717–22)

Here the effect is a heightening even beyond the usual over-reaching of the comparisons; Egypt and Assyria, in competition to outdo each other, provide pressures of emulation at the base that push the more magnificent Pandemonium to an insane pinnacle.

An exception to Milton's comparative similes is a group that might be called centrifugal rather than centripetal; the images lead our attention outward into history, rather than backward toward the archetypes. These instances are not really metaphorical at all, but are treated by Milton as facts of history, though he may take issue with the chronology or interpretation provided by "erring" pagans. The most famous of the group is the story of Mulciber's fall in Book I; another is the identification of Ophion with Satan transformed in Hell.

> However some tradition they dispers'd
> Among the Heathen of thir purchase got,
> And Fabl'd how the Serpent, whom they calld
> *Ophion* with *Eurynome,* the wide-
> Encroaching *Eve* perhaps, had first the rule
> Of high *Olympus,* thence by *Saturn* driv'n
> And *Ops,* ere yet *Dictaean Jove* was born. (x.578–84)

This image is constructed in a perspective of three planes, and on each there is sketched, through the allusion, a picture of the disorder and rebellion that will re-enact in legend the archetypal revolt. Greater extension is achieved in the compact lines from Book XI where history is shut in a span as the three points for its circumference are indicated:

> [the angel] blew
> His Trumpet, heard in *Oreb* since perhaps
> When God descended, and perhaps once more
> To sound at general Doom. (xi.73–76)

The same ends are served by the group of similes in *Paradise Lost* where Milton read the book of nature instead of the book of legend. An example is his extended treatment of the fallen angels in the early books. Here the poet follows much the same technique, on a larger scale, that he used on the verbal level in building up his picture of the Abyss. Simile is added to simile until we can construct all the

meanings inherent in Satan's cohorts. Milton mixes historical and natural images; three of the latter, all of them
well-known, occur in Book I. We first see the fallen angels
lying "intrans't" on the burning lake:

> Thick as Autumnal Leaves that strow the Brooks
> In *Vallombrosa,* where the' *Etrurian* shades
> High overarch't imbowr; or scatterd sedge
> Afloat, when with fierce Winds *Orion* arm'd
> Hath vext the Red-Sea Coast, whose waves orethrew
> *Busiris* and his *Memphian* Chivalrie,
> While with perfidious hatred they pursu'd
> The Sojourners of *Goshen,* who beheld
> From the safe shore their floating Carkases
> And broken Chariot Wheels, so thick bestrown
> Abject and lost lay these. (i.302–12)

This is really a pattern of two concentric similes, "natural"
and Biblical. The allusion to Pharaoh's overthrow reminds
us that the constant outbreaks of evil in history, following
the precedent of the original rebellion in myth, will be
suppressed by further manifestations of eternal providence.
They may be conquered by the very same natural forces —
"fierce Winds" — that were originally stirred up to punish
Adam and Eve: "as fierce Forth rush the *Levant* and the
Ponent Windes" (x.703–4). Images of storm in *Paradise
Lost* are generally related to Milton's treatment of the sea as
a destructive element. The antithesis of both sea and storm
is the "good dry land" from which spring flowers and fruits,
the symbols of nature's creative power; here it appears as
"the safe shore" from which the sojourners watch the destruction of the destroyers. The historical reference illustrates,
finally, the manner in which Milton integrated his similes
into the larger mythical scheme. By using metaphorically
the re-enactments, in history and pagan myth, of primeval

events, he could extend the poem's reach into the temporal stage of the myth — man's pilgrimage on earth — while preserving his concentric, non-temporal plan.

The encircling figure of the fallen leaves in this passage, besides its pictorial and emotional accuracy, contributes another instance of the analogical effects of the Fall, this time in nature. Sir Maurice Bowra, in showing that "the comparison of spirits in the underworld to fallen leaves is of great antiquity," lists instances from Bacchylides, Virgil, Dante's *Inferno,* and Tasso.[4] In Milton's poem, the ancient image takes on a special poignancy and terror, because the remote occasion of all these falls — of spirits, men, leaves — is to be explored. The falling leaves signify the "change Of Seasons to each Clime" (x.677–78) wrought in the natural world by the sin of men. The autumnal leaves of the simile exemplify our present distance from the Garden where Spring and Autumn once danced hand in hand. This is not to say that all the associations brought up here were present in Milton's mind when he wrote. But the analogy between the year's death and human death had given the image its power in classical times; Milton wrote of the event that brought Death into the world in all its forms, and made the comparison possible. The idea of barrenness, consistently associated with death and evil in *Paradise Lost,* generates many of the images for the fallen angels and the landscapes of Hell. Pharaoh's stricken hosts clearly belong to this complex of images and ideas.

Two other early similes for the fallen angels have counterparts in the final books of the poem, when natural evils overwhelm mankind. In making these subterranean analogies, like underground rivers flowing for many books beneath the poem's surface, Milton is working out his prem-

4 C. M. Bowra, *From Virgil to Milton* (London, 1945), pp. 240–41.

ise that what appear to be many different themes and legends
are in fact one. Here, the likeness between the first and
second Falls, of angels and men, is once more underlined.
The gathered troops of Satan are a blasted forest —

> yet faithfull how they stood
> Thir Glory witherd. As when Heavens Fire
> Hath scath'd the Forrest Oaks, or Mountain Pines,
> With singed top their stately growth though bare
> Stands on the blasted Heath. (i.611–15)

In this image there is the same combination of splendor and
desolation that has already been noted in Milton's briefer
phrases. The withered glory, like the fallen leaves, shows
that withering and death are the inevitable results of evil;
in imagistic terms, that Hell is unfruitful. The lightning-
struck trees anticipate the effect of the first lightning seen
by fallen man, when at the end of Book X Adam marvels at
the flame of "slant Lightning" that kindles the pines (1073–6).
A third natural image is again combined with an incident
from history. The angels arise from the lake like

> a pitchy cloud
> Of *Locusts,* warping on the Eastern Wind,
> That ore the Realm of impious *Pharaoh* hung
> Like Night, and darken'd all the Land of *Nile:*
> So numberless were those bad Angels seen
> Hovering on wing under the Cope of Hell. (i.340–45)

The ostensible point of comparison is that both angels and
locusts were "numberless," but the simile's application is
far wider. In Adam's vision of the future, the actual plagues
of Egypt are shown, providing a structural link between the
two ends of the poem, and hinting that the earlier instance
is more than casual. As locusts, the angels become them-

selves the chastisers of evil, another example of God's power to use wickedness for good ends. The "pitchy cloud" bringing unseasonable night has two analogues. One is the image of Satan as the eclipsed Sun shedding "disastrous twilight" over the nations (i.594ff.): the feeling of ominous foreboding is the same in both. The foreboding is justified when a shadow is cast upon Adam's precarious Paradise, and he fearfully recognizes the sign of God's punishment:

> Why in the East
> Darkness ere Dayes mid-course? (xi.203–204)

Finally, the cloud from the simile in Book I makes a last appearance in Book XII as Michael tells of the "darksom Cloud of Locusts" descending on Egypt to "blot out three dayes" (85 ff).

These examples do not exhaust the historical similes introduced by Milton in Book I to reinforce the theme of the fallen angels' impact on the world of man. The inundations of catastrophe that have periodically overwhelmed the earth are represented in other images; for instance, the barbarian invasions of Europe, in a simile patterned once more on the negative comparison.

> A multitude, like which the populous North
> Pour'd never from her frozen loyns, to pass
> *Rhene* or the *Danaw,* when her barbarous Sons
> Came like a Deluge on the South, and spread
> Beneath *Gibraltar* to the *Lybian* sands. (i.351–55)

The complex associations evoked by this passage include the implied secondary image of the Deluge (in *pour'd* and *spread*), adding the emotions surrounding the greatest Biblical disaster to the implications of barren savagery in the major vehicle. From the standpoint of the simile — the Dark Ages — the Flood is a memory, in the scheme of the poem a forecast; so time is telescoped as the images are superimposed. There is also a dim reminiscence of the rebel angels congregating in the North. In addition, Milton's metaphor of Europe's "frozen loyns" is a kind of horrible parody on one of his favorite ideas, the fertility that comes from God and from God's symbol, the sun; it also anticipates the "perverse" breeding in Chaos (ii.625). The barrenness of the entire picture is reinforced in the geographical reference to a desert, the "Lybian sands."

Following this image, Milton alludes to the angels, marching "in perfect *Phalanx* to the *Dorian* mood" (i.550), and a few lines further on, he joins all the warlike descendants of the angels who appear in fable and epic. The giants of Greek myth, Homeric heroes, Saracen invaders, and more gracious knights — all are to be later discarded, with their "long and tedious havoc," as fit subjects for an heroic poem (ix.27 ff.), so their association here is not surprising. Milton's final opinion of warfare comes in a prophecy of Michael, making the heroes of battles seem not very different from the locusts — "Destroyers rightlier call'd and Plagues of men" (xi.697).

The figure of the locusts was a favorite with Milton when he dealt in his prose with other "plagues of men." *Of Reformation* includes a prayer to the Trinity in which the offending churchmen are compared to wolves and wild boars, and finally to the locusts of Revelation ix.

O let them not bring about their damned designs, that stand now at the entrance of the bottomless pit, expecting the watchword to open and let out those dreadful locusts and scorpions, to reinvolve us in that pitchy cloud of infernal darkness, where we shall never more see the sun of thy truth again, never hope for the cheerful dawn, never more hear the bird of morning sing.[5]

The sentence provides an interesting and eloquent example of Milton's habit (it was, indeed, a habit of his age) of seeing even in the events of his own time diminished reflections of the superhuman actions embodied in the Christian myth. In *Paradise Lost,* the episodes that in prose appear as metaphors are set in perspective as parts of the universal scheme; in the middle distance is the "darksom Cloud" descending as a plague on Egypt, and in the foreground of Book I, the bottomless pit itself, opening to let out the "pitchy cloud" of demons. The sun of truth and the cheerful dawn are traced back to the mornings of Eden, with perhaps also an echo from a simile in Hell, where "wished Morn delayes" (i.208). The same conjunction of images turns up in another pamphlet; Milton is again castigating the Bishops:

Their covetousness and fierce ambition . . . as the pit that sent out their fellow-locusts, hath been ever bottomless and boundless.[6]

Anyone who investigates *Paradise Lost* with the other poems and the prose close at hand will have forced upon him an awareness of Milton's remarkable imaginative consistency. A few themes preoccupied him, though among them they summed up many of the perplexities of man's life; a few dominant images, on which infinite variations might be played, were used to express them. *Paradise Lost* grew fittingly and necessarily from the matrix of this imagination.

The last simile of Book I is that of the elves "in midnight Revels, by a Forrest side." Although it is much more charming in tone than the preceding examples, and is intro-

5 *SM,* p. 468.
6 *Tenure of Kings and Magistrates, SM,* p. 774.

duced chiefly to diminish the size of the angels, it supplies
another example of the superstition and false belief that
followed the loss of truth by man. Its appropriateness is not
immediately evident, but these reveling fairies recall the
other revels, portrayed by Milton in all their ominous beauty,
in *Comus*. There, too, there are "pert Fairies" and "dapper
Elves,"

> Yet have they many baits, and guilefull spells
> To inveigle and invite th' unwary sense
> Of them that pass unweeting by the way. (537–39)

The unweeting passer-by may be the "belated Peasant" of
Paradise Lost. Despite the Virgilian echo that gives the passage a kind of pathos, and the undeniable beauty of the image,
its context and the habitual association of its elements are
against it; it must be set (as Milton surely intended) on the
side of the fallen, not the faithful. Milton's attitude toward
fairies resembled, it may be, that of his peasant whose joy
was mixed with fear. The forest, moreover, has a sinister
connotation in *Paradise Lost*, as in the earlier poems; it is
like the enchanted wood of *Il Penseroso*, "where more is
meant then meets the ear" (120). The uncorrupted wood of
Paradise is usually qualified to make it more tame — for
instance, as a "spicie Forrest" (v.298); the labyrinth "of shrubs
and tangling bushes" (iv.176) that impedes Satan's way into
the Garden is of a more familiar kind. At the end of the
poem, the pleasant stand of trees in Eden has become "these
wilde Woods forlorn" (ix.910); they provide sanctuary for
the serpent and guilty man.

> O might I here
> In solitude live savage, in some glade
> Obscur'd, where highest Woods impenetrable
> To Starr or Sun-light, spread thir umbrage broad,
> And brown as Evening. (ix.1084–88)

The interaction here of forest and light imagery echoes Spenser's description of the Wood of Error, "not perceable with power of any starr" (*FQ*, I.i.7). The ramifications of this image can be pursued at length through most of Milton's writings; it is a useful example in showing that his individual symbols do not stand alone, but are backed by the convictions of his whole poetic life as well as by history, myth, and epic precedent.

Fairies and elves are minor instances of demonic power at work in the world; less cozy examples are the gods of the false religions, subjects of the major digression in Book I. Like the Mulciber passage, this is not figurative, but is accepted as fact, at least within the world of the poem. Since all history was potentially contained in the mythic events of the main plot, sub-plots in the form of historical allusion lead inevitably back to it, or are inevitably suggested by it. Thus, "the Streets of *Sodom*" (i.503), the Tower of Babel, and a dozen other symbols of confusion are held in solution in the imagery of Milton's first books. But in the long roll call of the pagan gods, confusion itself, in the shape of the fallen angels, is shown let loose on the world. Milton had used the idea earlier, in the *Nativity;* it was traditional and widely accepted in his time. It is the supreme instance of Satan's infiltration of a fallen race; and, planted in the midst of lesser images, this long account spreads its influence backward and forward through Book I, to lend historical authenticity to the other analogies between the fallen angels and the myriad plagues of men.

The many repetitions, at the end of *Paradise Lost*, of incidents foreshadowed in Book I — pagan gods flit in and out of Book XII, for example — answer Johnson's demand that the epic poet organize his work around "retrospection and anticipation." The plan also echoes the (perhaps fortuitous) one of the Bible itself, where the opening books provide symbols for the Apocalypse. Mr. Rajan says that "these huge similes reaching both backwards and forwards, with all space and all history caught in their towering span, have about them some quality of superhuman permanence." [7] In his figures for Satan's hosts in Books I and II, Milton lays the foundation for this towering span. Neither the fallen leaves nor the plague of locusts, nor most of the other images, is fully effective until we complete our knowledge of *Paradise Lost* and its myth.

IDEA AS IMAGE

Milton's epic similes are loopholes into history; they allow us to see the archetypes surrounded by their ectypes. As we read, we find the poem's texture thickening, though not changing radically in quality, at these points, taking on added dimensions and a new perspective. One step down from these full-scale comparisons with their widely-ranging allusions, we can find in *Paradise Lost* a wealth of lesser images, often undeveloped, where the references are rather to Milton's private "tradition": a body of imagery, woven through the earlier poems and the prose, that seems to have had special significance for him, finally reworked for its definitive incarnation in the great epic's mythic universe. An instance already touched on is the forest/labyrinth group.[8] These images reflect, often, the well-known motifs of anthropology and legend, gaining added symbolic power from their contact with extra-personal meanings.

---

[7] B. Rajan, *Paradise Lost and the Seventeenth Century Reader* (London, 1947), p. 124.

[8] For an examination of Milton's use of the labyrinth image, see G. Wilson Knight's essay, "The Frozen Labyrinth," in *The Burning Oracle* (London, 1930). He sees in mazes "an important symbol (to be found throughout Milton) for distress and confusion" (p. 62).

The recurrent images in the prose that reappear in *Paradise Lost* indicate that Milton, even when he handled the tools of practical discourse, chose certain ones with particular readiness. In the prose, they are mainly vehicles for metaphors; in the myth of the poem, they become properties with a real life within the poetic world, but they often bear the traces of their metaphorical life in an expressive potency and compactness. Thus the antagonists of the epic are shadowed forth by Milton in prose phrases like "the bright countenance of Truth"; in the poem, we are allowed to approach the Countenance itself, dazzling and dark with excessive bright, and summing up in itself all its figurative uses. So it is with much of the prose imagery: the figures of rhetoric are later shown to have their base in the nature of *Paradise Lost*. The flowers that symbolize the harmonious pastoral world of earth in *Lycidas* make a metaphor that goes one step further in *Areopagitica:* "this flowery crop of knowledge and new light"; there is a further metaphorical extension in "that undeflowered and unblemishable simplicity of the Gospel"; [9] and in Eden itself flowers, light, innocence and simplicity merge in archetypal images that demonstrate the essential unity of all these notions.

The complex of images clustered around the ideas of simplicity and confusion, and the rescue of simplicity from confusion, is a significant one for the epic and will repay some detailed inspection as an example, since there are interesting analogues in the imagery of Milton's other writings. In a passage from *Of Reformation,* the opponents of truth lurk in a plumbless depth of obfuscating confusion that foreshadows the "vast unbottomed infinite abyss" inhabited by monsters, in the epic. The muddy waters are symbolic of the obscurity that counters divine Truth.

[9] *Reason of Church Government, SM,* p. 536.

They [the Churchmen] fear the plain field of the Scriptures: the chase is too hot; they seek the dark, the bushy, the tangled Forest, they would imbosk: they feel themselves struck in the transparent streams of divine Truth, they would plunge, and tumble, and think to lie hid in the foul weeds, and muddy waters, where no plummet can reach the bottom. But let them beat themselves like Whales, and spend their oil till they be dragged ashore.[10]

It is a fine chain of association: from forest and stream to weedy shallows, ocean, whale, and the witty turn on *oil;* and is evidence, if evidence is needed, that the rapid, spark-striking revolutions of the imagination's inventive power were quite familiar to Milton. It is a power exercised, however, more widely in the prose than in the epic, where he is concerned to give us the unmistakable ancestors of these transparent streams and tangled forests. Chaos, grandfather of all images of confusion, also lurks behind much of the prose imagery, though it is not a presiding deity.

Whatsoever time, or the heedless hand of blind chance, hath drawn down of old to this present in her huge drag-net, whether fish or sea-weed, shells or shrubs, unpicked, unchosen, those are the fathers.[11]

This chaotic conglomeration fished from the nameless depths is not unexpectedly contrasted with "the plentiful and whole-some fountains of the Gospel," which, like the "transparent streams" of Truth, reflected the purity that Milton loved and "the fountain itself of heavenly radiance" where the nation was to be purged of error; they are all followed to their source in *Paradise Lost,* in the "pure Ethereal stream" of aboriginal light — "Whose Fountain who shall tell?" (iii.7–8).

[10] *Of Reformation, SM,* p. 453.
[11] *Of Prelatical Episcopacy, SM,* p. 470.

Milton's consciousness of antagonistic principles at war in the world is reflected in his pictures of Creation as the division of Chaos and the assigning of "like things to like" — a process invoked for analogy whenever the ordering power of God is the subject.[12] In an interesting sentence from *The Doctrine and Discipline of Divorce,* Milton remarks that God's activity, even in a fallen world, brings "due likenesses" together, while the work of the Devil is to confuse unlikes, and so inflame the "enmities of nature."

There is indeed a two-fold Seminary, or stock in nature, from whence are derived the issues of love and hatred, distinctly flowing through the whole mass of created things, and . . . God's doing ever is to bring the due likenesses and harmonies of his works together, except when out of two contraries met to their own destruction, he moulds a third existence; . . . it is error, or some evil Angel which either blindly or maliciously hath drawn together in two persons ill embarked in wedlock the sleeping discords and enmities of nature lulled on purpose with some false bait, that they may wake to agony and strife.[13]

The equation of harmony with the company of likes, and of warfare and agony with evil mixtures, is supported in the events and imagery of *Paradise Lost.* Casual metaphors are dramatized in mythical action. Thus, Milton conducts a prose argument, later in the divorce pamphlet, against "compelling together unmatchable societies," by referring to the Creation and Last Judgment:

Or if they meet through mischance, by all consequence to disjoin them, as God and Nature signifies, and lectures to us not

----

12 Cassirer writes, on the image of creation in mythical thought: "Emergence from the vague fullness of existence into a world of clear, verbally determinable forms, is represented in the mythic mode, in the imagist fashion peculiar to it, as the opposition between chaos and creation." *Language and Myth,* p. 81.

13 *SM,* p. 592.

only by those recited decrees, but even by the first and last of all
his visible works; when by his divorcing command the World first
rose out of Chaos, nor can be renewed again out of confusion,
but by the separating of unmeet consorts.[14]

The common belief in "Natures mystick Book" as the source
of "lectures" is evident here; but the particular nature invoked is now invisible to mortal sight, the subject of *Paradise
Lost*. There, the Last Judgment is almost always linked to
images of purification; we remember one of Milton's early
essays on the subject, when the Elder Brother of *Comus*
promised:

> But evil on it self shall back recoyl,
> And mix no more with goodness, when at last
> Gather'd like scum, and setl'd to it self
> It shall be in eternal restless change
> Self-fed, and self-consum'd. (593–97)

Metaphorical allusions to "purging" and "separating" become real in the framework of pre- and post-historic events,
where the last shall be like the first: a state of purity and
simplicity succeeding the confusions of history. The hell-
hounds of *Paradise Lost,* Sin and Death, are assigned to

> lick up the draff and filth
> Which mans polluting Sin with taint hath shed
> On what was pure. (x.630–32)

They are then, "cramm'd and gorg'd," to be sealed up in
Hell,

> Then Heav'n and Earth renewd shall be made pure
> To sanctitie that shall receive no staine. (x.638–39)

The Last Judgment, as the Bible assures us, will be followed
by still another creation, which this time will remain pure

14 *Ibid.*

forever. Dissolution of what has been corrupted, the refin-
ing-out of a new world, just as the earlier one "rose out of
Chaos," is predicted; the Savior is

> to dissolve
> *Satan* with his perverted World, then raise
> From the conflagrant mass, purg'd and refin'd,
> New Heav'ns, new Earth, Ages of endless date. (xii.546–49)

The phrasing suggests a deliberate parallel with the Creation,
where dregs are "downward purg'd" and "like things to like"
ordained (vii.234, 240). Satan's efforts are directed toward
muddying the pure waters of paradisal existence, an attempted
dissolution of it into Chaos. They are followed by little
repetitions of the creative act, as "unmeet consorts" are
once more divided by God. Before the War in Heaven, Christ
promises that he will,

> Armd with thy might, rid heav'n of these rebell'd,
> To thir prepar'd ill Mansion driven down
> To chains of Darkness, and th' undying Worm.
>
> .   .   .   .   .
>
> Then shall thy Saints unmixt, and from th' impure
> Farr separate, circling thy holy Mount
> Unfained *Halleluiahs* to thee sing. (vi.737–44)

The prediction takes effect, and Adam after the event
marvels at

> the evil soon
> Driv'n back redounded as a flood on those
> From whom it sprung, impossible to mix
> With Blessedness. (vii.56–59)

Even Belial, in his speech to the assembly in Pandemonium,
realizes that the inevitable result of an attempt to corrupt

Heaven will be the unmixing of the mixed, the sorting out
of "due likenesses."

> Yet our great Enemie
> All incorruptible would on his Throne
> Sit unpolluted, and th' Ethereal mould
> Incapable of stain would soon expel
> Her mischief, and purge off the baser fire
> Victorious. (ii.137–42)

Satan's attempts to confuse the orderly creation are most
successful in his corruption of Adam and Eve. The Fall of
Man was a regression of distinct, clearly separate, *named*
entities, to their origin in the nameless confusions of primeval being, symbolized by our loss of the beasts' names in
a confusion of tongues. After the Fall, man's state resembled
Chaos. The desire of Adam and Eve to be as gods upset
the proper order of things, just as Satan's rebellion had done
in Heaven. Their *hubris,* which they imagine to be a step
toward godhead, is accomplished by a disturbance of natural
equilibrium that results in the very thing they wish to tran-
scend: chaos. This is the irony in tragedy, where the hero's
gesture toward the stars upsets his balance, produces anarchy,
and ultimately delivers him to the chaotic powers of darkness.
Just so, when man's fatal decision has been made in *Paradise
Lost,* strife and consequent reconstruction follow. The
Redemption of Man is to be a purging off of old corruptions,
the restoration of a clarity that is at once new and very
old. But first he must be separated from the stainless ground
of Eden, and Milton uses a familiar image as God judges:

> Those pure immortal Elements that know
> No gross, no unharmoneous mixture foule,
> Eject him tainted now, and purge him off
> As a distemper, gross to aire as gross,

> And mortal food, as may dispose him best
> For dissolution wrought by Sin, that first
> Distemperd all things, and of incorrupt
> Corrupted. (xi.50–57)

Imagery of purging, evil mixtures, disease, and dissolution,
link the passage clearly with others on the same theme; and
again the ideas of harmony and purity merge as the negatives
of both are rejected. The "dissolution wrought by Sin" is
death: it is a melting of the ordered organism back into the
chaos whence it came. Dissolution turns up again in Book
XII, with the prophecy that Christ will "dissolve *Satan* with
his perverted World" (xii.546–47). Then will come man's
"tribulation," to prepare him for re-creation.

> Tri'd in sharp tribulation, and refin'd
> By Faith and faithful works, to second Life
> Wak't in the renovation of the just . . . (xi.63–65)

An examination of these linked passages and their re-
hearsals in Milton's prose reveals the actions of mind and
spirit, expressed in metaphor, transformed to veritable
physical action in the imagery of a hierarchical universe. The
difference between Milton's procedure in *Paradise Lost* and
other procedures perhaps more familiar and acceptable to us,
can be further developed if we look at another image of disorder in Book IX. The storms that rage through the early
books, and overtake fallen Nature after man has sinned, have
their analogues in the sinners.

> They sate them down to weep, nor onely Teares
> Raind at thir Eyes, but high Winds worse within
> Began to rise, high Passions, Anger, Hate,
> Mistrust, Suspicion, Discord, and shook sore
> Thir inward State of Mind, calm Region once
> And full of Peace, now tost and turbulent. (ix.1121–27)

Here is the reverse of the process by which the Son once brought peace from the troubled deep. It has already taken place in Satan; his mind is like the waters of Chaos, "up from the bottom turn'd by furious windes":

> Horror and doubt distract
> His troubl'd thoughts, and from the bottom stirr
> The Hell within him. (iv.18–20)

The peculiar virtues and uses of Miltonic imagery (which are, of course, not the only poetic virtues) can be seen more clearly if we contrast these lines with a similar Shakespearean image from *Troilus and Cressida*.

> My mind is troubled, like a fountain stirr'd;
> And I myself see not the bottom of it. (III.3)

Even in this minor instance, we catch something of Shakespeare's infinite suggestiveness; it is the meditation of Achilles, hero and no hero, unable to fathom the depths of his own nature, who will kill the clear-sighted, truly heroic Hector. Indeed, one might say that the play's bitter taste is localized here, and the marvelous capacity for making concrete in this way a whole range of ideas is one of the sources of Shakespeare's power. Nevertheless, if one can make the point without seeming to despise his method, his metaphors are in the philosophical sense accidental, while Milton's are based on analogies of substance — are, therefore, not truly metaphorical at all. Even when Shakespeare's figures are deeply imbedded in the verbal texture, we are usually conscious of making implicit comparisons, of "joining a plurality of worlds." [15] The joining gives new insight into all the worlds

15 This "poetry of association by comparison" is contrasted by René Wellek and Austin Warren with "poetry of association by contiguity, of movement within a single world of discourse." *Theory of Literature* (New York, 1949), p. 200.

concerned; if the metaphor is right, it actually creates significance, producing relationships where we saw none before. The terms of the comparison merge to point toward a new, complex meaning, whose total appropriateness to the context makes us call it unique, to echo Emerson's phrase, "a new thing." But the simile for Achilles' mind is "accidental" in that it is a construct, designed to project a further significance; his mind is not actually a fountain. Shakespeare used also, of course, traditional analogies based on the "Elizabethan world picture," but in them, too, the areas of comparison (for example, the civil and natural hierarchies in the king/ sun metaphor) are parallel rather than concentric. Milton's worlds all fit exactly inside each other; in noting their points of similarity, he is not so much joining different objects as observing the same thing on a smaller or larger scale. Because the same forces operate in all parts of a self-consistent, mutually dependent universe, the images may be used interchangeably for what we should now separate into "subjective" and "objective" situations.

Satan's mind is *really* a Hell, the exact reflection or diminished replica of the "place of doom obscure and foule" from which he comes. And the winds contending in the soul of Adam are real winds — not, perhaps, gusts of moving air, but manifestations of a force identical with the one that impels the storms in the natural world. The winds that stir his soul are from an older time than we know, when *pneuma,* the breath of Heaven, was the principle of life for body *and* soul, for the world's body and the body of man. All this is really a repetition in a new context of a point made often before: that Milton's world, because it is mythical, is still a *single* world, within which metaphor, as we know it, is irrelevant. Mrs. Langer has spoken of the "identification of fact, symbol, and import, which underlies all literal belief in myth," [16] and it is this unity that makes us feel, in reading *Paradise Lost,* that we are observing familiar forces operating in different physical areas, rather than comparing similar areas in different hierarchies or "worlds." The image of the disruptive storm which can be followed through the poem resembles three overlapping planes of a painting, or three concentric sections of a cone. They are: "actual" mythical events in the external world, for example, the upturned waves of Chaos; "actual" mythical events in the internal world, for example, Adam's tossed and turbulent thoughts; and thematic repetitions of these events in history, for example, the eruption of Mt. Aetna. The technique brings Milton closer to "primitive" direct experience than any other English poet except Blake, who wrote "mythologically" too, though his myth was a heresy. Shakespeare's metaphors are revelatory, restoring lost unities in imagination; with him, we strike through our present chaos to a temporary order. Milton's are reportorial, as though he were presenting us with an existing situation; with him, we stand inside an order before it has been rendered transitory, or above it, to observe its underlying eternal patterns.

In the group of images examined in the first section of this chapter, Milton combines various analogies that all point to a single complex idea as their tenor (the fallen angels); in the storm imagery leading up to the "tost and turbulent" mind of fallen man, a single complex image directs our attention, through a constant analogy between vehicle and tenor, to the same forces at work in many different instances. The first arrangement is horizontal, the second vertical. In both, the vehicles of the similes are simply less grand and general instances of the archetypes; the barbarian hordes are not "really" fallen angels, but they admit a true parallel because

[16] *Feeling and Form,* p. 186.

they represent the counterpart in history of a mythic event. The same causes are in play, and the same results follow. Both trains of imagery do much to establish, obliquely, Milton's major theme, to imbed in the poem's very texture the dire "change" of man's fall which transformed eternity into time and the archetypes into the bewildering shapes of history.

"THE FAULTLESS PROPRIETIES OF NATURE"

There is in *Paradise Lost,* finally, an imagery of the surface, in which the persons and places of the poem are directly characterized. "Imagery" becomes a misleading term here because it usually suggests, first, metaphor, and second, visual impressions. Milton's descriptive imagery, as we have already observed, is not fundamentally metaphorical; it is also, frequently, non-visual, because the incarnate abstract qualities of his "properties" were as important as visible concrete ones. Nevertheless, the descriptive surfaces of the poem must be called imagery, since their function is to acquaint us with concrete individual entities.

The most important of these "individuals" are the three areas of Milton's stage: Heaven, Hell, and the Garden. Paradise is situated halfway up the pyramid; it is the scene of the poem's crucial action, the most intimate and universal of all archetypes. The soul longs to return whence it came, and the impulse persists even when the science of origins has changed our name for the source, so that our remembrance of things past leads to the womb and not to Paradise regained. Several critics have noticed that the approach to Milton's Paradise resembles a dream, in which an ancient pattern is re-enacted.

The physical situation of Adam and Eve . . . symbolises the security of their innocence, their happy unawareness of the forces of good and evil which war on the perimeter. Milton presents this still centre, with its womb-like security, in such a way as to stir the unconscious memory of every reader. His Paradise is our first world, dangerless and unsmirched as it is seen by a child. . . . Only dreams can open those gates. . . . The Garden of Eden is in fact a dream world, in that it is the scene for the enactment of a collective dream or myth embodying the psychological experience of the race.[17]

Though the assumptions about human nature implied in this paragraph would have been foreign to Milton, it indicates the profound reverberations set up by this particular archetypal idea even in a secular modern consciousness.

Milton's view of nature in Eden is based on a venerable idea at least as old as ancient Egypt, and perhaps as old as man: the concept of nature as organism. The systems based on this concept survived, with necessary modifications, through the Christian era and up to the later seventeenth century, even as the mechanistic cosmology that was to replace them was gaining strength. Although Milton made Raphael divide the chain of being into the conventional categories of vegetal, sensitive, and rational souls, his nature in *Paradise Lost* often comes close to pre-Christian vitalism and to older mythical versions of nature's body in primitive legend. As Cassirer says of mythical thought: "Wherever it finds an organically articulated whole which it strives to understand . . . it tends to see this whole in the image and organization of the human body." [18] The organic quality of Milton's world is revealed by Raphael:

> For know, whatever was created, needs
> To be sustain'd and fed; of Elements
> The grosser feeds the purer, earth the sea,
>   .   .   .   .   .

17 Mahood, *Poetry and Humanism*, pp. 180–81.
18 *Mythical Thought*, p. 90.

> The Sun that light imparts to all, receives
> From all his alimental recompence
> In humid exhalation, and at Even
> Sups with the Ocean. (v.414–26)

This is more than a simple anthropomorphism; it is the deeply-felt embodiment of an idea; though admittedly a pseudo-scientific diction here robs it of some of its effect. Milton went further, with better effect, in a later passage. A nineteenth-century mythographer complained that primitive man "attributes sex and procreative powers even to stones and rocks, and he assigns human speech and human feelings to sun and moon and stars and wind." [19] Milton's sun, at noon, shoots "down direct his fervid Raies, to warme Earths inmost womb" (v. 301–2); and later, Raphael amplifies:

> Other suns perhaps
> With thir attendant Moons thou wilt descrie
> Communicating Male and Femal Light,
> Which two great Sexes animate the World,
> Stor'd in each Orb perhaps with some that live. (viii.148–52)

The concept of the two great sexes explains the complementary roles of earth and sun; the sun, when Satan visits it in Book III, is metallic and mineral — made of gold, silver, carbuncle, chrysolite. The earth, however,

> may of solid good containe
> More plenty then the Sun that barren shines,
> Whose vertue on it self workes no effect,
> But in the fruitful Earth; there first receavd
> His beams, unactive else, thir vigor find. (viii.93–97)

Living things of the lower orders are endowed with feelings and even a kind of consciousness; the "happie Constella-

19 Andrew Lang, *Myth, Ritual and Religion* (2 vols., London, 1901), I, 49.

tions" and the flora and fauna of Eden rejoice at the marriage of Adam and Eve. The physical world of *Paradise Lost* is a thoroughly animated one, by the standards of latter-day anthropology, or of classical cosmology.

Milton's belief in an organic universe, though certainly not unique in his century, was supported in his poetry with unusual consistency and conviction. It sprang from his insistence, shared by "primitive" myth-makers and by certain strains in the Christian tradition, on seeing the external world as permeated with value and meaning. One of the greatest of all values for him was fertility, the creative potency that imitates the boundless fecundity of God. In *Comus,* he had exalted "the sage and serious doctrine of Virginity"; but even there, the Lady praises "Natures full blessings," and virginity is hardly visible in the abundant nature of *Paradise Lost.* Discussing the attributes of God in the *Christian Doctrine,* Milton places first among those "which show his divine power and excellence," the idea of *Vitality,* and interprets with persistent literalness the Scriptural phrase, "the living God." [20] His deity is the Creator above all; the aptest epithet for his devil is the Destroyer. The contrast between the powers of life and the forces of death controls much of the language of the poem that at first glance might seem casual or conventional: the "fruits of joy and love," the Sun's "sovran vital Lamp" (iii.21), and Milton's provocative placing of words like *withered* and *faded* in the early passages on the fallen angels. The angels were once (and are still called by Satan) "the Flowr of Heav'n" (i.316); in the same vein, we hear always of *vales* and *fields* of Heaven, a fertile countryside contrasting with the sterile landscapes of Hell; there the angels walk "by living Streams amid the Trees of Life" (v.652), but Hell is "a Universe of death . . . Where all life

20 I, ii. *SM,* p. 926.

dies, death lives" (ii.622–24). This view is in the great tradition, shared by both classical and Christian humanism,
which held that life itself is a good, and the goodness of God
manifest in the lives of his creatures. Attached to its roots is
a still more primitive feeling, the instinct for survival itself.

On the other hand, the fecundity of created nature is not
unchecked by rule; rather Chaos, the home of elements warring to the death, is the type of disorder. Milton's nature and
its consummation, the Garden of Eden, must combine vitality and pattern if it is to be faithful to his scale of values.
These two are united in only one kind of being known to us:
the living organism. The characteristics of organic nature,
Susanne Langer has said, are "self-preservation, self-restora-
tion, functional tendency, purpose."

> Life is teleological, the rest of nature is, apparently, mechanical.
> . . . Only organisms have needs; lifeless objects whirl or slide
> or tumble about, are shattered and scattered, stuck together,
> piled up, without showing any impulse to return to some pre-
> eminent condition and function. But living things strive to
> persist in a particular chemical balance, to maintain a particu-
> lar temperature, to repeat particular functions, and to develop
> along particular lines.[21]

The idea that inorganic nature, as well as its visibly living
parts, is also "alive" and directed by purpose, malignant or
benevolent, is a feature of most mythologies, though animism
was under-emphasized by Christian theology, as bordering
too closely on pantheism. But to Milton the aliveness of the
universe was a congenial and necessary postulate.

> *Adam,* thou know'st Heav'n his, and all the Earth:
> Not this Rock onely; his Omnipresence fills
> Land, Sea, and Aire, and every kinde that lives,
> Fomented by his virtual power and warmd. (xi.335–38)

21 *Feeling and Form,* p. 328.

The happy Garden, center of God's overflowing goodness, could hardly, therefore, be pictured otherwise than as a living body. C. S. Lewis has called attention to the "hairie sides" of the mountain that help to establish the image as we approach.[22] Once inside, we find a being with its own metabolism. The organic imagery of Eden, as well as its timelessness, makes necessary Milton's stress on cyclical patterns in Paradise; the life of a vital being moves in recurrent rhythms of systole and diastole, extension and contraction, activity and rest. The beneficent interchange of opposites is appointed for men in the cycle of "labour and rest," and for nature as well in a cyclical course of need and refreshment.

> Southward through *Eden* went a River large,
> Nor chang'd his course, but through the shaggie hill
> Pass'd underneath ingulft, for God had thrown
> That Mountain as his Garden mould high rais'd
> Upon the rapid current, which through veins
> Of porous Earth with kindly thirst up drawn,
> Rose a fresh Fountain, and with many a rill
> Waterd the Garden. (iv.223–30)

A sense of profusion runs through the fifty lines of Milton's introduction to Paradise, an easy abundance projected through the physiological vocabulary and the underlying image of organism. "Sweet is the breath of morn, her rising sweet," says Eve; and the soft breathing of Eden weaves itself into other key images.

> The Birds thir quire apply; aires, vernal aires,
> Breathing the smell of field and grove, attune
> The trembling leaves. (iv.264–66)

William Empson has remarked that these lines contain "a

---

[22] *A Preface to Paradise Lost* (London, 1942), p. 47.

serious secret pun"; [23] they also contain, in marvelously telescoped though not very secret form, three different image-
strands, all important for Milton's larger picture. One is
organic, again: taking *airs* as the winds that are actually the
breath of the Garden. Another is music, and a third, the
sweet smell that seemed to come into Milton's imagination
at once when he thought of Paradise. The "native perfumes"
of Eden meet Satan as he approaches and provide an oppor-
tunity for the image of Araby the Blest. The Creator himself finds the incense from Eden's flowers "grateful" (ix.197);
and Eve walks "veild in a Cloud of Fragrance" (ix.425), a
concentration of the pure and perfect air surrounding her.

Paradise is not only a vital world, "answering the great
Idea" of its Creator's infinite vitality; it is also the product
of the archetypal creative process that divides the abyss so
that harmony may be possible. Augustine's remark that "the
world's beauty . . . [is] composed of contraries, not in figure
but in nature," finds its fulfilment in Milton's Eden. Life is
generated by the command of the creative Word to the
"fertil Womb" of earth; earth itself is a marriage of unlikes,
a varied landscape patterned on reciprocity and alternation:

> sweet interchange
> Of Hill and Vallie, Rivers, Woods and Plaines,
> Now Land, now Sea, & Shores with Forrest crownd. (ix.115–17)

The balance of opposites underlying this countryside —
"this variety . . . Of pleasure situate in Hill and Dale" (vi.
640–41) — takes shape at the Creation, when the emergence
of hills is answered by the hollowing of the valleys.

> So high as heav'd the tumid Hills, so low
> Down sunk a hollow bottom broad and deep. (vii.288–89)

23 *Some Versions of Pastoral* (London, 1935), p. 159.

The river whose underground course ends in a rising fountain continues its progress in division and reunion.

> And now divided into four main Streams
> Runs divers, wandring many a famous Realme.
>   .   .   .   .   ..
>   meanwhile murmuring waters fall
> Down the slope hills, disperst, or in a Lake,
> That to the fringed Bank with Myrtle crownd,
> Her chrystall mirror holds, unite thir streams.
>   (iv.233–34, 260–63)

This river, with its variety and unity, is the backbone of Milton's description in the fourth book; tracing its passage through the Garden, he gathers all the delights of Paradise. The importance of fountains, rivers, and "rills" for Milton, and their contrast with the destructive salt sea, has been noted; their freshening power is here traced to its source in the veins that nourish Eden. The vital spirits, too, become the "breath" of the body's rivers, the blood; for Milton's microcosm/macrocosm relation works in both directions:

> Th' animal Spirits that from pure blood arise
> Like gentle breaths from Rivers pure. (iv.805–6)

Eden and its inhabitants are swayed by the same forces.

Arnold Stein has observed that in Milton's first description of Eden there is a balance between light and dark, open field and unpierced shade; the light imagery of *Paradise Lost* is, of course, part of the pattern of ideas and images that conveys the cosmic war of creation against destruction, and is woven into the contrast between dead and living matter.

[Milton's Paradise] is a compressed myth of natural sympathy and order, between light and darkness, between the waters below and the waters above; growing things are blessedly in the center, thirsting downward for darkness and earth and water, thirsting upward for light and sky and water.[24]

The picture satisfies all our sympathies and impulses; ourselves growing things, a mixture of opposites, we need all four elements, and our Paradise is a world where earth and the underground waters are still innocent, the dark descent fertilizing rather than destructive. Above all, Milton's account shows us an organism, "the semblance of life, or activity maintaining its form." [25]

Nature does not, of course, remain innocent in *Paradise Lost*. The underground river ends in the allusion to the gathering of Proserpina by Dis, king of an underworld of terrors. The ancestor of Dis, Satan, is already in the Garden, risen from regions of death Greece never knew. In Book IX, it is not only the serpent who becomes the corrupted vehicle for his destructive ends. To enter the Garden, Satan uses the very river whose sweet alternations delighted us in Book IV; the parallel to that vision is this:

> There was a place,
> Now not, though Sin, not Time, first wraught the change,
> Where *Tigris* at the foot of Paradise
> Into a Gulf shot under ground, till part
> Rose up a Fountain by the Tree of Life;
> In with the River sunk, and with it rose
> Satan involv'd in rising Mist. (ix.69–75)

The precariousness of his Paradise is suggested by Milton repeatedly, from the moment when assault on it is suggested in Beëlzebub's hint that "this place may lye expos'd" (ii.360). It does, indeed, lie exposed, in innocent vulnerability. As

---

24 Arnold Stein, *Answerable Style* (Minneapolis, 1953), pp. 65–66.
25 Langer, *Feeling and Form*, p. 67.

Satan approaches from Chaos, it is "this frail World" (ii. 1030); his first view is of something tiny and dependent:

> And fast by hanging in a golden Chain
> This pendant world, in bigness as a Starr
> Of smallest Magnitude close by the Moon. (ii.1051–53)

The Earth is God's bauble, fitting spoil for the first thief. Milton adds to the sense of frailty with his reference to the least of stars, and the phrase "close by," as the little world (whether earth or star) hovers and shelters near a neighboring body. Once on earth, we find, despite the enclosed bliss of the Garden, "in narrow room," a kind of openness, the frankness of innocence and uncorrupted generosity; it is "to all delight of human sense expos'd" (iv.206) — and thus exposed, too, to Satan. This vulnerability is, of course, the physical counterpart of Milton's moral fable where man, endowed with free will, must stand alone, unsupported save by his freedom. Eve argues that Eden (and man) must have been created by God *able* so to stand, not subject to corruption.

> Fraile is our happiness, if this be so,
> And *Eden* were no *Eden* thus expos'd. (ix.339–41)

But frailty and exposure are, in fact, the condition of man and his dwelling place. Adam answers, "within himself The danger lies" (348–49); just as, within the depths of Paradise, there is a darkness capable of corruption, making creation, in a sense, "imperfet."

Eden is ruled jointly by order and abundance, which in our fallen experience often clash. In Paradise, the disorder of too much abundance, which Milton drew so powerfully in *Comus,* is still potential; there is, however, the ghost of a suggestion that its richness is inordinate. Take the much-admired lines on the "Virgin Fancies" of unfallen nature,

> pouring forth more sweet,
> Wilde above rule or art; enormous bliss. (v.296–97)

A poet obliged to depict the inconceivable richness of Eden probably could not avoid some such extravagance as this, and it succeeds magnificently. Still, Milton was always conscious of the root meanings of his Latin words, and intended them to be operative in the poem. In *enormous,* he has reiterated the idea that paradisal nature was "above rule." *Rule* is a potent word in *Paradise Lost;* it is used of the angels who rule "each in his Hierarchie, the Orders bright" (i.737), but above all of God:

> *Confusion* heard his voice, and wilde uproar
> Stood rul'd, stood vast infinitude confin'd. (iii.710–11)

And Adam's rule is to be a smaller replica of his Creator's. References to his gardening mention the "wanton growth" of branches, and the need to "reform Yon flourie Arbors" (iv.629, 625–26), with at least an undertone of double meaning in *reform.* Eve's argument for working alone is based on the widespread disorder of the Garden, and she echoes Adam —

> One night or two with wanton growth derides
> Tending to wilde. (ix.211–12)

Adam is more moderate: "our joynt hands Will keep from Wilderness with ease" the exuberant growth (ix.244–45); but the idea that the wilderness is there, waiting to encroach at the slightest neglect, remains. This submerged suggestion of unruly nature is a very minor current in Milton's total picture of Paradise. Its chief effect is to enhance the power and wisdom of Adam, *ruling* the wilderness. The notion of order as something positive and created, to be maintained by effort of will, is consonant, however, with Milton's general view of the contending forces in the universe, and with one strenuous strain in Puritanism. It does not, of course, involve the belief that nature is evil — only that the creature is necessarily less complete than the Creator, and so, vulnerable to evil. An angel points out that the stars prevent the recapture of "her old possession" by Night (iv.666); and the moon, too, "in her pale dominion checks the night":

> th' other Hemisphere
> Night would invade, but there the neighbouring Moon
> (So call that opposite fair Starr) her aide
> Timely interposes. (iii.725–28)

Again, the picture is of earth as something frail and threatened. The idea of encroaching night seems, ironically, to have been early in Milton's mind; in a Latin exercise, he had praised the sun as the "means of staying the lapse of all things into the primeval Chaos." [26] The alternation of day and night, sun and moon, rising and setting, that is part of the paradisal order, is an exquisitely poised balance of opposites, and thus precarious. The sense of danger is part of the emotive effect Milton wished to build up in *Paradise Lost;* it is accomplished partly by these hints of powerful natural forces, uncertainly held in check, on the borders of life.

On the whole, however, the happy gardens of the poem — paradisal and heavenly — provide an answer to the dilemma posed in *Comus* between nature's "full and unwithdrawing hand" and the "holy dictates of spare Temperance." Milton, when he wrote his masque, could not quite manage

[26] *Private Correspondence*, p. 61.

to dramatize an alternative to Comus' rich description that would seem more than an equally undesirable extreme — though the legendary gardens of the Spirit's Epilogue suggest a synthesis and resolution. Fallen nature is, indeed, made up of extremes. In unfallen Paradise, however, and in the Elysian flowers and amber streams of Heavenly fields, the abundance of "enormous bliss" is matched by the clarity and purity of a positive temperance: "such concord is in Heav'n" (iii.371).

The force of Books IV and V is great, even when they are read alone; but they never should be read alone, and are meant to be seen against the background of Hell, from which we have risen in the first books. The breathing airs, the spicy woods, moist earth and fresh vegetation of Eden are the positive equivalents of Hell's negations. The image-pattern — river, organism, scents, dance, fertile growth — constructed for Paradise is matched by a cluster of baleful images characterizing Hell. Two solid "places" are thus given shape and distinctively set off against each other to make visible two opposing forces. Critics who have complained that the typical note of Miltonic imagery is sounding brass are justified if they confine their attention to the first two books and the sixth. Milton is reproducing here "Noise, other then the sound of Dance or Song" (viii.243), and his imagery is tuned to it. The similes for the fallen angels, sharing the quality of destructiveness, reflect (or are reflected by) the barren waste of their "ill Mansion." They are surrounded by what St. Paul called "the unfruitful works of darkness." [27]

The positive side of his universe is shown by Milton not only in Book IV, but in the account of Creation in Book VII, where he expands and exploits, with a characteristic literal-

[27] Ephesians, 5:11.

ness, the suggestions of Genesis, where earth was commanded
to "bring forth" the creatures.

> The Earth obey'd, and strait
> Op'ning her fertil Woomb teem'd at a Birth
> Innumerous living Creatures, perfet formes. (vii.453–55)

Milton's whole description of this scene has a deliberately
naive freshness and charm; it is the product of his belief,
more or less literal, in "Earth all-bearing Mother" (v.338).
The contradiction of this fecundity is given body in Book I,
where there is not a single image, scarcely a single word, that
suggests anything organic, until the simile of "thundring
Aetna."

> Whose combustible
> And fewel'd entrals thence conceiving Fire,
> Sublim'd with Mineral fury, aid the Winds,
> And leave a singed bottom all involv'd
> With stench and smoak. (i.233–37)

The conception and the entrails, however, are a dreadful
mockery of true fertility; breeding in Hell, as Milton tells
us, is "perverse." The image is modulated immediately into
the inorganic metaphor of a chemical reaction (*sublim'd*).
A few lines later Satan, surveying his kingdom, asks: "Is this
the Region, this the Soil, the Clime . . . That we must change
for Heav'n?" *Soil* and *clime* do not deceive us, however, since
we have just been shown that this soil is really a "singed
bottom." Satan's "Farewel happy Fields" supplies an unhappy reminder, in the single word *fields*, of the fertility that
he has left behind for the "dreary Plain forlorn and wild,"
the "bare strand" of the dolorous regions. Milton maintains
a counterpoint between the harsh inorganic imagery of Hell
and the remembrance, in allusions to light and freshness, of

what has been lost; it is the imagistic equivalent of his linguistic contrasts between *then* and *now*. Satan's summarizing speech in Pandemonium contains a series of antithetical images.

> We may chance
> Re-enter Heav'n; or else in some milde Zone
> Dwell not unvisited of Heav'ns fair Light
> Secure, and at the brightning Orient beam
> Purge off this gloom; the soft delicious Air,
> To heal the scarr of these corrosive Fires
> Shall breath her balme. (ii.396–402)

Light, safety, and the mixed sensuous appeal for touch, taste, and smell of the soft, delicious, and balmy air, are to balance the gloom, the unhealed wounds, the wasting fire.

An apparent contradiction to the prevailing imagery of the early books is the simile in Book II where the angels' reaction to Satan's resolve is described as a moment of brightness after storm. The impermanence of the scene, in the wide waste of Hell, is striking, and it is enhanced when one realizes what the image is doing. It transports the fallen angels, for an instant, to the place from whence they fell, or at least to the near-heavenly landscape of Paradise. The image is tuned to Milton's major pastoral mode: gentleness, freshness, abundance, music.

> If chance the radiant Sun with farewell sweet
> Extend his ev'ning beam, the fields revive,
> The birds thir notes renew, and bleating herds
> Attest thir joy, that hill and valley rings. (ii.492–95)

Revive and *renew* are key words; Paradise is briefly regained by the fallen. The image confirms an irony if it is seen against the other great picture of Satan as the sun, in Book I. There, Milton gives him as he actually is, his glory obscured;

the later image, whose function is to show his followers' wishful deluded idea of him, is of a potent, revivifying sun, recovered from his terrible eclipse.

The section in Book II where the fallen angels explore their new abode — "that dismal world" — makes a parallel for Milton's long description of the Garden in the fourth book. The rivers of Hell, infernal counterparts of the "four main Streams" in Paradise, are *baleful, deadly, rueful;* Acheron, "black and deep," contrasts with the streams of Eden and Heaven that run clearly over the sands and flowers visible at the bottom. The frozen continent beyond is made up of lifeless molecules like those in the description quoted earlier, that "whirl or slide or tumble about, are shattered and scattered, stuck together, piled up."

> Beyond this flood a frozen Continent
> Lies dark and wilde, beat with perpetual storms
> Of Whirlwind and dire Hail, which on firm land
> Thaws not, but gathers heap, and ruin seems
> Of ancient pile: all else deep snow and ice,
> A gulf profound . . . (ii.587–92)

The air is not odorous and warm, but *parching* — an epithet already used potently in *Lycidas* to convey destruction, with a hint of unfulfilled need. The sweet interchange of opposites in Eden, where shade follows sunlight and both are benevolent, is replaced by

> the bitter change
> Of fierce extreams, extreams by change more fierce,
> From Beds of raging Fire to starve in Ice. (ii.598–600)

The "wish and struggle" of the damned is far removed from the perfect fulfilment of life for Adam and Eve.

If the key image of Paradise is the clear river, the corre-

sponding one in Hell is fire. The flames of Hell to us may be
a worn-out metaphor; but no Puritan preacher ever brought
them to life with more persistence and ingenuity than Milton
in Book I of *Paradise Lost*. Fire is not, however, merely the
décor of Hell; it is chiefly important as the destructive principle itself, and as such it is a continuing thread in the poem,
when Hell goes out to attack the innocent. It is regularly associated with the sonorous, metallic imagery for which Milton
is famous, and often with images of violation and disorder.
The building of Pandemonium provides a first instance of
its malignant power.

> There stood a Hill not far whose griesly top
> Belch'd fire and rowling smoak; the rest entire
> Shon with a glossie scurff, undoubted sign
> That in his womb was hid metallic Ore,
> The work of Sulphur. (i.670–74)

The pronoun *his* for *womb,* though an accepted seventeenth-
century substitute for the neuter pronoun, nevertheless sets
the soil of Hell sharply apart from "mother Earth," and suggests something of the unnaturalness of the process that is
to follow. Milton extends the suggestion with one of his
sudden excursions into history, as men become the pupils of
Mammon:

> By him first
> Men also, and by his suggestion taught,
> Ransack'd the Center, and with impious hands
> Rifl'd the bowels of thir mother Earth
> For Treasures better hid. Soon had his crew
> Op'nd into the Hill a spacious wound
> And dig'd out ribs of Gold. Let none admire
> That riches grow in Hell; that soyle may best
> Deserve the pretious bane. (i.684–92)

The impiety here is of the worst sort: it is unnatural,
unkindly, an incestuous violation of order. Pandemonium

itself is all unnatural, an imitation of the spontaneous beauties of Heaven. Milton's references to art are frequently pejorative; the flowers of Paradise are the products, not of "nice Art," but of "Nature boon" (iv.241–42). Eve works with "such Gardning Tools as Art yet rude Guiltless of fire had formd" (ix.391–92). Fire, its products, and its powers, are alike "guilty" in *Paradise Lost*.

As for gold, Milton saw it most often, with medieval eyes, as something unfruitful, and so belonging to death. He was not immune to traditional accounts of golden pavements in Heaven; but when placed in a favorable light in *Paradise Lost*, gold is usually (not always) modified into an adjective, *golden*, or surrounded by organic imagery — or even made organic itself, as in the famous "vegetable gold." [28] Milton's general rule, when he is using any metallic or mineral imagery for his Heavenly landscapes, is to add some qualifying epithet: the gates of Heaven, made of "Diamond and Gold," are called "living dores" (vii.566), the battlements constructed "of living Saphire" (ii.1050). As the phrase "precious bane" suggests, however, gold, outside the safe circle of Heaven, is more often destructive or barren than profitable; in the account of the golden calf, it is linked again with disease:

> Nor did *Israel* scape
> Th' infection when their borrow'd Gold compos'd
> The Calf in *Oreb*. (i.482–84)

Gold is associated, finally, with the underground regions of its origin, and so with the dark and dangerous.

The War in Heaven is related to the accompaniment of

---

28 Mr. Bush has shown that in this phrase, "each word is altered and quickened by the other," *vegetable* softening "the idea of unhealthy artifice and evil which in *Paradise Lost* is associated with gold." *Paradise Lost in Our Time* (Ithaca, 1945), p. 95.

the loud martial music, the disorder, and the flames that we have come to associate with Hell itself. The association is made possible, in the first place, by Milton's anti-chronological plan, which allows Hell to establish itself imaginatively *before* the War is related. So in Book VI, the rebels in the north inhabit "a fierie Region" (vi.80), that is both preview and echo of their doom to come; when the battle begins, "all Aire seemd then Conflicting Fire" (vi.244–45).

> So under fierie Cope together rush'd
> Both Battels maine, with ruinous assault
> And inextinguishable rage. (vi.215–17)

Fire and rage are identified as inner and outer aspects of the same force; these angels are the ancestors of the choleric man of medieval psychology, whose personality was formed by the element of fire. The noisy conflict of fire with fire is hushed when the Son enters; he has much the same effect on the little chaos created by the war as he is to have later on the endless warfare of the greater Chaos. The change brings images of order and freshness.

> At his command the uprooted Hills retir'd
> Each to his place, they heard his voice and went
> Obsequious, Heav'n his wonted face renewd,
> And with fresh Flourets Hill and Valley smil'd. (vi.781–84)

Order itself is interpreted as the return to proper places and qualities (the "wonted face" of Heaven), the two essentials that are always carefully established in Milton's epithets and images.

Satan's invasion of the "Ethereous mould" of Heaven in Book VI is an analogue to the construction of Pandemonium when the soil of Hell was rifled.

> Which of us who beholds the bright surface
> Of this Ethereous mould whereon we stand,

This continent of spacious Heav'n, adorpd
With Plant, Fruit, Flour Ambrosial, Gemms & Gold,
Whose Eye so superficially surveyes
These things, as not to mind from whence they grow
Deep under ground, materials dark and crude,
Of spiritous and fierie spume, till toucht
With Heav'ns ray, and temperd they shoot forth
So beauteous, op'ning to the ambient light.
These in thir dark Nativitie the Deep
Shall yeild us, pregnant with infernal flame. (vi.472–83)

It is a speech characteristic of Satan, and its full meaning
emerges in the light of the mythic images Milton has been
constructing in the first half of the poem. In a world without
sin, "bright surfaces" reflect the essences of archetypal beings;
they are sharp, simple, unmistakable, instantly visible. This
is the first time that a survey of them has been called superficial; there is no such thing as superficiality in a world of
Platonic essences, but Satan invents it by distinguishing
between the surfaces and the elements "from whence they
grow." Surface and implied depth are complementary aspects
of single beings whose source is God, properly regarded, but
Satan's dark imagination insists on tearing the two apart and
exploring the depths alone. He is already busy making a
Hell of Heaven; already, to him, it is a Deep full of infernal
flame. Following this speech comes a scene of violation, a
disturbance of natural process like the spacious wound that
revealed earth's gold.

In a moment up they turnd
Wide the Celestial soile, and saw beneath
Th' originals of Nature in thir crude
Conception; Sulphrous and Nitrous Foame
They found, they mingl'd . . .
Part hidd'n veins digged up nor hath this Earth
Entrails unlike) of Mineral and Stone. (vi.509–17)

All this is accomplished, of course, "ere day-spring" (521),

since light is averse to such doings. Fire and light are contrary elements sprung from a common root, or destructive
and creative aspects of one original energy; Milton's use of
them is like his contrast between destructive sea and pure
river. The chaotic entrails of the soil are turned to good
when "toucht With Heav'ns ray"; but the cannon's fuse is
"pernicious with one touch to fire" (vi.520).

It is, perhaps, odd to find the soil of Heaven hiding these
pernicious elements. But Milton, throughout the poem,
shows a troubled distrust of the unformed potentiality of
nature, even while he admits its necessity; and it is a vein
that seems to be continuous through his universe. "Th' originals of Nature" dug up by Satan are related to the elements
in Chaos, where he found all things "in thir pregnant
causes mixt Confusedly" (ii.913–14). A little chaos is thus
allowed to make part even of the brilliant actuality of Heaven
— which is, after all, not identical with God, and must
therefore partake of imperfection. Earth and Heaven are,
indeed, "Each to other like, more then on earth is thought"
(v.576). The materials dark and crude are not products of
Satan's imagination, but objects of his attention; they *are*
there, marring the complete clarity of Heavenly being. Their
fearsomeness is in part simply the result of their being
hidden, as the "hidden lustre" of gold is dangerous (ii.271).
In *Paradise Lost,* of course, this problem cannot be stated,
as it was by Spenser and Shakespeare, in terms of appearance and reality; everything in this world is a reality. It is,
rather, a question of potentiality (the deep is *"pregnant* with
infernal flame") and actuality, and the proper places of
things. Only God is pure actuality; the Creation will never
be completely realized.

So, as the points of Milton's compass direct us to Heaven
and Hell, on a smaller scale a glance upward or downward
will reveal quite different aspects of God's world, and each

area of the great stage turns out to be a microcosm of the whole. Everything depends on the way we choose to turn our glance: up toward the light, or downward with Satan. Like nature in Eden, the lower elements of the universe are not evil; but their formlessness is a sign of the imperfection that makes them vulnerable to the uses of evil as well as good; even the underground river in Paradise provides a channel for the entrance of Satan. The hidden veins of Heaven's soil, left to themselves, flower into beauty and virtue, as they are "tempered" by the light of the upper world. Untimely ripped from their natural places by Satan, they take on the explosiveness of disordered being.

Whenever, therefore, Milton prepares to explore the underground regions in *Paradise Lost,* we become aware of a sense of danger. They are, in the first place, always dark, and so a function of one of Milton's primary symbols. Thus, the War in Heaven, at its climactic moment, is made to take place in a shadowy "underground"; the incident of the uptorn mountains is not only a bow to classical precedent, but creates in "reality" the situation that it "symbolizes," the staining of Heaven's purity by sin. The hurtling hills make a proper abode for the abysmal contending powers:

> So Hills amid the Air encounterd Hills
> Hurl'd to and fro with jaculation dire,
> That under ground they fought in dismal shade. (vi.664–66)

The persistent association of evil with the underground makes even the description of the sun's action in the depths of earth take on an ominous coloring.

> Th' Arch-chimic Sun so farr from us remote
> Produces with Terrestrial Humor mixt
> Here in the dark so many precious things
> Of colour glorious and effect so rare. (iii.609–12)

The major intention is to praise; but there is a verbal echo of the precious bane of Hell, reinforced by "here in the dark." A similar undertone can be heard in the account of the underground rivers' origin.

> But they, or under ground, or circuit wide
> With Serpent errour wandring, found thir way,
> And on the washie Oose deep Channels wore. (vii.301–303)

The word *error,* like the "mazie error" of Book IV, is still innocent. Nevertheless, for us in history, *error* has other meanings, and the epithet *serpent* is not irrelevant to them.

For us, Milton's double-sided universe will suggest its analogues in the geography of man's soul: the conscious and unconscious regions of the mind, and the principles of order and anarchy that live there; in other language, the abyss in the heart of which Augustine spoke. Milton's care in revealing the places of darkness is consistent with his world-view, which was dynamic and moral always. Struggle, temptation, resistance, were everywhere, imbedded in the very structures of macrocosm and microcosm. The constant presence of some sort of "abyss" in *Paradise Lost* is a reminder that the possibility of a fall is never far away. The inclusion of a darkness in the very midst of light is, too, appropriate to the tensions of a mythic world where all the events of history are held in embryo.

To the images of the underground river and the hidden veins of earth, may be added the ocean of *Paradise Lost,* in its various incarnations. The primeval sea is Chaos itself; it harbors, traditionally, a monster or serpent. "The bottom of the monstrous world" visited by Lycidas is seen in prototype in Milton's epic as another incarnation of the lower regions where the powers of destruction lurk. The destruction may be controlled by a divine power, but it is no less terrible for that, and stirs some of the fears in the very depths of our nature.

> All dwellings else
> Flood overwhelmd, and them with all thir pomp
> Deep under water rould; Sea cover'd Sea,
> Sea without shoar; and in thir Palaces
> Where luxurie late reign'd, Sea-monsters whelp'd
> And stabl'd. (xi.747–52)

In myths of the hero, the night journey is followed either in (or on) the sea, or into the depths of the earth, and the monster is usually encountered in these fearful regions. Any "unknown" territory may serve as the setting for these adventures: "desert, jungle, deep sea, alien land"; [29] but all share either the physical strangeness of the dark, or the spiritual strangeness of alien places, or both. The duel that takes place is a struggle between two powers, one the inhabitant of the underworld, the other an antagonist from the regions of light. The two direct encounters in Christian myth between Christ and Satan take place in a wilderness and in Hell when the Harrowing is accomplished. A psychological "explanation" for all these underworld adventures and battles, encountered by Hercules, Odysseus, Jonah, and any number of other heroes, is based on the idea of a return to the world we knew before birth; the journey is followed by a "rebirth" in which the secrets of the deep are brought back to be used for the benefit of man, that is, a more complete understanding of the self.

Theseus and Peirithous . . . descended into Hades and grew fast to the rocks of the underworld, which is to say that the conscious

---

[29] Campbell, *Hero with a Thousand Faces*, p. 79.

mind, advancing into the unknown regions of the psyche, is overpowered by the archaic forces of the unconscious: a repetition of the cosmic embrace of Nous and Physis. The purpose of the descent as universally exemplified in the myth of the hero is to show that only in the region of danger (watery abyss, cavern, forest, island, castle, etc.) can one find the "treasure hard to attain." [30]

One need not accept this interpretation uncritically in order to see its relevance to Milton's version of the universal myth in *Paradise Lost*. His three-tiered stage includes a Chaos that holds literally "archaic forces" and regains some territory in nature and man at the Fall. The minds of Adam and Eve are "tost and turbulent" when sin invades them; Adam is "in a troubl'd Sea of passion tost." After the Fall they hide themselves in "the thickest Wood," which is not only the wood of Genesis, but an image for darkness and confusion persistent in Milton. The Fall of Man can be interpreted physically as the encroachment of Chaos on Creation, psychologically as the descent of the conscious mind into the unconscious, or spiritually as the dislocation of God's natural hierarchy of sense, will, and reason. The same images can accommodate all three. Since the Fall, the troubled sea has been part of human history, as sea monsters usurped man's dwellings at the time of the Deluge; and of the human personality, so that complete self-knowledge demands a descent into it — as Milton suggested in another context in *Areopagitica*.

The haunt of "the dragon that is in the sea" is always dark, formless, archaic. Satan and his followers assume its colorings, absorbing the manifold images of the destructive and rebellious monsters of legend, sea or earth-born. Dagon, the opponent of Samson, is "Sea Monster, upward Man And down-

---

[30] Jung, *Psychology and Alchemy*, p. 322.

ward Fish" (i.462–63). Satan is the serpent slain by Apollo, or his ancestor:

> Now Dragon grown, larger then whom the Sun
> Ingenderd in the *Pythian* Vale on slime,
> Huge *Python*. (x.529–31)

He is also Ophion, conquered by Saturn, and, most notoriously:

> In bulk as huge
> As whom the Fables name of monstrous size,
> *Titanian,* or *Earth-born,* that warr'd on *Jove,*
> *Briarios* or *Typhon,* whom the Den
> By ancient *Tarsus* held, or that Sea-beast
> *Leviathan,* which God of all his works
> Created hugest that swim th' Ocean stream. (i.196–202)

The constant association of these creatures with "places" of destruction, strife, and sin, gives them a characterizing function similar to that of Milton's weather, flora, and landscape.

Shot through the contrasting regions of the epic, then, is a balance between an upper world of air and purity, and a hidden, monster-haunted world of dark perplexity. The conflict between darkness and Milton's powerful living light pervades most of these contrasts and is, of course, his most potent instrument for making concrete the drama of *Paradise Lost:* the struggle of opposites that brings about the Fall and, ultimately, the Redemption.[31] In the poem, light is hardly ever used as a mere vehicle, as it had been in the prose, where Milton wrote, for example, "Truth is as impossible to be soiled by any outward touch, as the sunbeam."[32] The

---

[31] It is also one of the key points of reference in Milton's architectural structure. "The development of the mythical feeling of space always starts from the opposition of *day* and *night, light* and *darkness.*" Cassirer, *Mythical Thought,* p. 96.

[32] *Doctrine and Discipline, SM,* p. 574.

light of *Paradise Lost,* in mythical fashion, sums up many
such ideas; it is the source of life, of purity, of truth, and in
itself contains them all. It is an actor in the drama, a substantial quality that participates as ruler of the upper regions, life-bringer, truth-revealer, the purger of mists from
inner and outer sight.

To a blind man, light would naturally have a special
poignant appeal; but even in his youth, Milton had felt its
power with particular force. One of the most suggestive lines
in the early poems is a prayer to the Moon, to

> visit us
> With thy long levell'd rule of streaming light. (*Comus,* 339–40)

In this line, light is already associated with a web of allied
ideas that might be called "abstract"; its straightness is contrasted with the crookedness of the "leavie labyrinth," its
"rule" with the lawlessness of Comus' dark orgies. Milton's
image is actually a matter of perception rather than invention. Light really does travel in a straight line — is, indeed, a
standard of straightness. It is also necessary for the performance of any precise and controlled action (taking *rule* in its
other meaning). As Milton wrote in his early exercise,
"Whether Day or Night is the more excellent": "Day serves
for use as well as pleasure, and is alone fitted to further the
business of life." [33]

In the epic, light absorbs also the group of ideas connected
with fertility and vitality. It is habitually associated with
"fresh dews" and the revival of life after night or storm. The
passages that describe the coming of night in Eden have a
serene loveliness, but only because we know that morning
will surely follow. It is the dawn, "sure pledge of day" (v.168)

[33] *Private Correspondence,* p. 61.

that holds the purest joy, and the rising of light in Paradise is always attended by a burst of gratitude. The long passage in Book V when all the creatures of the Garden give thanks to the author of light, is a mosaic of light-imagery shot through with the gladness of the morning. One of the few places in *Paradise Regained* where we hear again the music of *Paradise Lost* is the passage after the storm in Book IV, where Milton brings together a group of images made familiar in the earlier poem: on one hand, the winds rushing out from "stony caves," uprooted trees, the fearful din of "Infernal Ghosts"; on the other, the fair morning, the fresh vegetation, the cheerful sun and the songs of birds as they "gratulate the sweet return of morn" (*P.R.*, iv.438).

The warfare of light against darkness is made explicit and literal in Milton's language on several occasions, as in the invocation to light:

> Before the Heavens thou wert, and at the voice
> Of God, as with a Mantle didst invest
> The rising world of waters dark and deep,
> Won from the void and formless infinite. (iii.9–12)

And a few lines before, the triumph of light's rule over Chaos has been celebrated as Satan approaches the universe.

> But now at last the sacred influence
> Of light appears, and from the walls of Heav'n
> Shoots farr into the bosom of dim Night
> A glimmering dawn; here Nature first begins
> Her fardest verge, and *Chaos* to retire
> As from her outmost works a brok'n foe
> With tumult less and with less hostile din. (ii.1034–40)

"Shoots" leads into the military figure, and also recalls the long levelled rule; its suggestion of powerful action recurs later, when the sun "shoots invisible vertue even to the deep" (iii.586). Old Night, the "Anarch," is ruler of a frontier that is "encroacht on still through our intestine broiles" (ii.1001) — the incessant battle with the forces of light. In Adam's conversation with Eve about the stars, the implications for life and death of the dark/light antithesis is made clear.

> Ministring light prepar'd, they set and rise;
> Least total darkness should by Night regaine
> Her old possession, and extinguish life
> In Nature and all things, which these soft fires
> Not only enlighten, but with kindly heate
> Of various influence foment and warme,
> Temper or nourish, or in part shed down
> Thir stellar vertue on all kinds that grow
> On Earth, made hereby apter to receive
> Perfection from the Suns more potent Ray. (iv.664–73)

The fires of the stars are modified by *soft*, a term habitually used by Milton in association with life, particularly in Paradise. Light is related, of course, always to *one* of the two basic dimensions of *Paradise Lost,* height and depth. Although there are supposed to be no directions in Chaos, Milton aligns his source of light definitely with the "upper" regions. Satan suggests as much in two echoing lines where we can hear also the voice of another pilgrim, earlier in historic time, but a successor in mythical time, Aeneas:

> Long is the way
> And hard, that out of Hell leads up to Light. (ii.432–33)

The sun, chief organ of light to earth-dwellers, is an actor in *Paradise Lost,* and also a source for similes — a dual role made possible by the qualities of Milton's world that are really and essentially shared, not brought together tem-

porarily by the poet. The most effective figure for Satan in
the early books explains his fallen state in terms of light
imagery: it is "Glory obscur'd."

> As when the Sun new ris'n
> Looks through the Horizontal misty Air
> Shorn of his Beams, or from behind the Moon
> In dim Eclips disastrous twilight sheds
> On half the Nations, and with fear of change
> Perplexes Monarchs. Dark'n'd so, yet shon
> Above them all th' Arch Angel. (i.594–600)

This darkening is the outward and visible sign of Satan's
inward and spiritual disgrace. The "disastrous twilight" foreshadows the catastrophic gloom of the Fall; it is one of
Milton's major anticipations. The monarchs perplexed by
fear become, *sub specie aeternitatis,* Adam and Eve bewildered by the heavy change of death. In addition, something
is added to our notion of "dark" itself. It now means not
only "absence of light and goodness," but fear — and fear is
one of the passions unfelt until the Fall, unknown to Paradise when we first enter it. But the central image is the most
important. Satan is the sun; only he is a sun "shorn of his
Beams," and thus impotent, as Samson shorn of his hair was
helpless. In the context of *Paradise Lost,* this impotence can
be taken literally. The beams of the sun are the organs whose
"gentle penetration" conveys life to the world (iii.585), but
Satan can no longer give life. He inhabits instead "a universe
of death." The real sun "dispenses Light from farr" (iii.
579); in his effortless strength, he is Lord of the sky. But
Satan can only "shed" fear, not "shoot" virtue. The misty air
he looks through would be melted away by the actual, potent
"Celestial light," to whom the poet prays: "all mist from
thence Purge and disperse" (iii.53–54). The contrast be-

tween this picture of Satan as an impaired source of light, and the true intact sources — God, or the sun — embodies precisely the relation between the poem's basic forces. A supplementary image is that in Book III as Satan approaches the actual sun; he becomes a blemish on its surface, a sunspot, spoiling its perfection as his own perfection was spoiled in the eclipse simile (iii.588–90).

The potency of Milton's light imagery, as well as the function it performs in his poem, can be illustrated by comparing a few lines with the corresponding place in Dryden's *State of Innocence*. Dryden's "opera" is focused on Adam and Eve, their follies and humors; most of the supernatural "machinery" is omitted, and with it the mythical points of reference that gave Milton's drama its meaning. The opening scene, however, is in Hell; Lucifer speaks:

> If thou art he! But ah! how changed from him
> Companion of my arms! how wan! how dim!
> How faded all thy glories are! [34]

The famous corresponding speech in Milton reads:

> If thou beest he; But O how fall'n! how chang'd
> From him, who in the happy Realms of Light
> Cloth'd with transcendent brightness didst out-shine
> Myriads though bright. (i.84–87)

The lines show Milton's habitual method of playing his images and archetypes against each other. The change of the fallen angel is described positively by a reminder of the realms from which he fell, a Marlovian dazzle of light that lifts us at once to the center of Milton's image and its meaning. In Hell, we are always aware of Heaven; in Heaven, we

---

[34] John Dryden, *Works*, ed. Walter Scott and George Saintsbury (18 vols., Edinburgh, 1882–93), V, 126.

look down on the deep tract of Hell. Dryden's lines work in one direction only; a pale negative impression, redundantly expressed, replaces Milton's energetic chiaroscuro.

In his major images, Milton creates a substance, and with it a meaning and a role, for the chief "places" of his poem. In his Hell of fire, rock, and "mineral fury," there is the violence and futile destructiveness of mindless inorganic nature untouched by the fertilizing power of light; in Paradise there is the body of life, a delicate, harmonious balance of fecundity and order; and through the universe run vertically the parallel and antithetical powers of light and darkness. All these trains of imagery are continued into history in the final books of *Paradise Lost,* as the wonders of Heaven and Hell come to inhabit earth and the heart of man. The panorama that Adam sees is chiefly a melancholy vision of waste and warfare, of "fruitless hours"; but there are some redeeming scenes. We are shown one dawn more glorious than all the mornings in Paradise:

> Ere the third dawning light
> Returne, the Starres of Morn shall see him rise
> Out of his grave, fresh as the dawning light. (xii.421–23)

God's creativity is exercised once more in the Redemption, and Adam's reaction to it brings the wheel of myth and imagery full circle:

> more wonderful
> Then that which by creation first brought forth
> Light out of darkness! (xii.471–73)

One of the most elaborate scenes in Michael's pageant is the episode of Noah, "the onely Son of light In a dark age" (xi.808–9), and his story is told in images that make the Deluge a repetition, in miniature, of the first Creation.

Michael himself tells Adam that, with the vision of the Flood, he has "seen one world begin and end" (xii.6) — and, presumably, begin again. As the water rushes down, Chaos, the original "sea without shoar," claims the earth again and the monsters of the deep inhabit human dwellings. The passage on the re-emergence of the land recalls the command of God on the third day:

> Be gather'd now ye Waters under Heav'n
> Into one place, and let dry Land appeer. . . .
> The watrie throng,
> Wave rowling after Wave, where way they found,
> If steep, with torrent rapture, if through Plaine,
> Soft-ebbing. (vii.283–300)

Now, the sun after the Flood draws away the water,

> which made thir flowing shrink
> From standing lake to tripping ebbe, that stole
> With soft foot towards the deep. (xi.846–48)

God's pledge re-establishes the order of nature, and with it the recurrent cycles that prevailed in Eden; though by now winter has made its appearance, and seasons are defined by the work done in them:

> Day and Night,
> Seed time and Harvest, Heat and hoary Frost
> Shall hold thir course, till fire purge all things new. (xi.898–900)

Counter to the forces of order are the warfare and hatred of the race of man. The consistency of Milton's imagery is nowhere better seen than in his depiction of the plagues of Egypt. Each of the elements has its mythical prototype in the books that have gone before, and the evil fortune of the

Egyptians is shown to be manifestly a product of the same self-destructive power that brought the fallen angels to their ill mansion. The rivers, always for Milton a sign of fertility (and especially so in Egypt), are turned to blood: life is spilled instead of nourished.

> Thunder mixt with Haile,
> Haile mixt with fire must rend th' *Egyptian* Skie
> And wheel on th' Earth, devouring where it rouls. (xii.181–83)

Here the "Whirlwind of dire Hail" in a Hell that reverberates with God's thunder is echoed; the locusts and the darkness follow, and the death of Egypt's first-born, the result of Sin "that first Distemperd all things" (xi.55–56). Pharaoh, the "River-dragon," is a descendant of the Leviathan of Book I, and he is finally devoured by his own element, as "the Sea Swallows him with his Host" (xii.195–96).

The individual images in the passage on Egypt are traditional; they are found in the Bible, and among the legends of disaster in other cultures. Milton's distinction is not that he characterized the elements of his myth in a new way, but that he succeeded in revealing so clearly the outlines of the universal themes behind them. The properties of *Paradise Lost* have not the beloved detail of our private precious objects; they have been given by the poet, instead, the intimate, well-worn outlines of the public mental landscapes that we walk in and touch every day. Not the thickness of individual denotation, but the density of endless implication, weights Milton's images. They contribute to the shapes and boundaries of the ideas we entertain, direct our seeing and our thinking; they have haunted our childhood, populated fairy tales and epics, and will accompany us till death: fire and water, sea and sky, rivers, valleys, hills and caves, sun and stars, garden and forest, night and day, deep Hell and high Heaven. They are not original with Milton, but the originals of much that he, and we, had read of and seen. We experience them with the carelessness of familiarity; in *Paradise Lost,* they resume their true gravity, clarity, and power.

VI

SATAN'S VOYAGE

In Books II to IV of *Paradise Lost,* Milton has given his version of one of the basic mythological themes: the quest, second stage of the "celestial cycle" of loss, search, and return. "The perpetual stumble of conjecture and disturbance in this our dark voyage" was portrayed earlier in the woodland wanderings of *Comus.* But the theme did not find its most profound incarnation until Satan voyaged out of Hell to light. His is a journey conjectural and disturbed enough, the original instance and subsequent type of fallen man's endeavor. Satan is the archetypal exile; the theme is transferred to man at the end of the poem, as the dark voyage of the race of Adam is adumbrated in the great panorama of Old Testament wanderings in the final books, which illustrate in history "the exile of temporal life."

Satan is not, obviously, *the* hero of *Paradise Lost.* But the story of his voyage is told by Milton *as if* he were one of the questing heroes of legend, while at the same time we are reminded of his position in the moral scheme of the poem as a whole. The elements of his character that Milton borrowed from heroic legend and epic link his adventures with those of the archetypal hero-figure; the elements that belong to the Devil of Christianity help us to see the hero himself in proper perspective, as one who makes the best of a fallen and sin-bound condition; though, once more, the short-comings of Satan's methods show up sharply against the humility and resolve of fallen Adam at the end of the poem. Heroism and heroic energy are virtues only in a world where struggle, doubt, and danger are real; one would not call the heavenly host heroic, nor God energetic. But Milton's epic, in its broad outlines, was to be a *complete* rendering of the types of human experience, and to be complete it had to include an account of life "as the state of man now is," as well as a picture of the happy state as it once was and a forecast of happiness to come. The life of fallen man could not, however, be enacted by a human hero, unless the poem's temporal and structural unity were to be sacrificed; Paradise knew nothing of the dark voyage. To show the results of the Fall graphically in the human offspring of Adam and Eve would have trammelled the poem with an unwieldy time-scheme and an inartistic break in the action.

Milton's solution shows an inspired simplicity. The dark voyage is transplanted to the life of the first fallen being.[1] Human pain, struggle, confusion, and (one must add) energy and courage, are brought together in a creature who, while not technically human, shares the relevant human condition: he is sinful and hedged about with limitations. Satan carries this theme, of faltering and seeking "natural man," until, after the Fall, Adam is ready to assume its burden. The hero of myth, it has been said,

---

[1] The same point can be made about the War in Heaven; war is the second prime symptom of the human condition, but inappropriate in Eden. Like Satan's journey, the heavenly war of Book VI is echoed in the conflicts of human history exhibited to Adam in Books XI–XII. It is less centrally pertinent to Milton's myth than the quest, but is included for similar reasons.

must be one who is sufficiently "human" to be imagined as rep-
resentative of mankind in its strivings and failures. Such are
Aeneas — Dante himself — Adam — Faust. It is perhaps the one
inherent weakness of Milton's myth that Adam, in his perfect
innocence and ignorance of evil before the Fall, is a figure so
remote from all our experience that it is well-nigh impossible
to invest him with real interest.[2]

This complaint is frequently lodged against Adam as hero.
But Milton, we may think, anticipated Adam's remoteness,
and so made Satan joint-hero of the poem, precisely because
he was "sufficiently human" to be recognized as an exemplar
of our predicament. After the middle of Book X Satan dis-
appears, his part ended, leaving Adam to suffer and contend
as the true wayfaring hero.

The continuous parallel between the fall of the angels and
the fall of man is, of course, one of the major structural and
moral principles of the poem; the imaginative linking of
Satan's "wandering quest" with our own fate as voyagers
through the unknown is, therefore, not difficult. Milton prepares us for this equation at the beginning of *Paradise Lost,*
through a gradual change in the tone of his descriptions of
Hell. Although, in the first part of Book I, the tone is one
of remoteness and terror, by the time the first book ends we
are feeling much more at home, among pilasters, Doric
pillars, and bossy sculptures; Pandemonium is all too like
the brassy and barren splendors of our own public occasions.
This modulation from the remote to the familiar has been
criticized as one of Milton's famous inconsistencies, but in
fact the angels must be brought closer to our own level if
we are to accept a quasi-identification between Satan and
ourselves. In Book I, the progression is deliberate and art-
ful; its hinge is the long account of the pagan gods, which

[2] Charles R. Buxton, *Prophets of Heaven and Hell* (Cambridge, 1945), p. 38.

brings the fallen angels literally into the context of the known world. When Pandemonium is likened to Babel, Babylon, and Cairo, the transition is almost complete, but it is advanced still further as Book II moves on. The soil of Hell in Book I has a nightmare ambiguity — neither land, liquid, nor fire; but in Book II the landscape takes on more familiar contours with the help of classical and Biblical reminiscences: it becomes "a frozen Continent" with "four infernal rivers." Inconsistent it may be; but, like the time-table in *Othello,* faithful to the psychological necessities of the poem.

The pastimes of Hell's inmates, once they have risen from the burning lake, are clearly human. The games, included principally to match the funeral games of ancient epic, and to point up the fruitless, frivolous nature of activity in Hell, also help to establish a parallel with the human or semi-divine heroes of myth. Two passages are especially pertinent. One is the section on the "vain wisdom" of the angels' philosophical discussions, which "found no end, in wandring mazes lost."

> Of good and evil much they argu'd then,
> Of happiness and final misery,
> Passion and Apathie, and glory and shame,
> Vain wisdom all, and false Philosophie. (ii.562–65)

Of these scenes in Hell, G. Wilson Knight remarks, "It is, indeed, our own fallen world that Milton depicts," and adds: "The Satanic party are mankind in its fruitless struggles." [3] It is always necessary, in reading *Paradise Lost,* to remember that Milton maintains almost constantly a dual point of view; he sees the world simultaneously from a vantage-point

---

[3] *Chariot of Wrath* (London, 1942), p. 137.

outside time, and from the dusty arena where the struggle is real, necessary, and an inevitable recourse of resilient if short-sighted human nature. Philosophy may be false, but humanity will go on philosophizing; struggle may be fruitless (though it is not always), but it will be engaged in as long as men exist. The angels' philosophy is, of course, especially vain because they are irredeemable, cut off hopelessly from good. But chiefly, in these lines, Milton is describing *human* preoccupations, including his own: good and evil, happiness and misery, glory and shame — they are the universal themes of legend and myth, of *Paradise Lost* itself. These mixed, opposing concepts are inevitably objects of speculation in a world where value and disvalue "grow up almost inseparably"; Hell is the first where such duplicity is known, but not the last. Two notes are struck in this passage: in the first three lines, a familiar one that brings us closer to a scene in which we (as Satan) are shortly to participate; and in the fourth line, the deeper tone of the timeless setting, where the vanity of these puny philosophers reverberates hollowly within the grand structure of universal truth. The double point of view is characteristic of irony, and the first three books of *Paradise Lost* together form one of the most sustained ironic passages in our literature. Irony is fundamentally tragic; it calls out simultaneously our sympathetic emotions and our critical intellects. Above all, the ironic vision of life refuses to permit a simple attitude. Hence, all arguments as to where our sympathies lie in the early books of Milton's epic are vain; they lie *both* with the follies of the fallen, and with the rigors of reason and discipline that are necessary for our salvation as reasonable beings.

The fallen angels, like fallen men, are wanderers in a maze, searching in vain for an end. From being wanderers in thought, they soon become wanderers in action:

> Thus roving on
> In confus'd march forlorn, th' adventrous Bands
> With shuddring horror pale, and eyes agast
> View'd first thir lamentable lot, and found
> No rest: through many a dark and drearie Vaile
> They pass'd, and many a Region dolorous,
> O're many a Frozen, many a Fierie Alpe,
> Rocks, Caves, Lakes, Fens, Bogs, Dens, and shades of death.
>
> (ii.614–21)

The geography has become even more recognizable, the entire picture miserably familiar. Mankind in the wilderness of the world views his lamentable lot with the same shuddering horror, passes through a "drearie Vaile" of tears; the dolorous regions form part of the scenery of Malory's melancholy magic world, of *Sir Gawain, The Faerie Queene, Pilgrim's Progress*. Everyman, like Hell's angels, traverses the valley of the shadow, though unlike them he may attain the Heavenly City. God's mercy and man's repentance add a new dimension to the fate of these angels, but they do not change the initial stages of the journey; the Slough of Despond has still to be crossed and the sickness unto death undergone. Milton's passage reproduces in small compass the wider voyage of Satan, where the true prototype of the dark journey will be enacted; it brings us to the very brink of the abyss where that voyage is to take place.

In both of the passages examined above, the fallen angels are seekers; in the first, for an "end" — both literally and teleologically — in the second, for rest. *Seek, find, discover, search:* these recur persistently in Milton's epic vocabulary. They point to the same goals nearly always: *rest, peace, ease.* The activities of Hell are a vain attempt to achieve quietness, each angel seeking "where he may likeliest find Truce to his restless thoughts" (ii.525–26). Behind *truce* are images of warfare and division that sprang to life when Heaven and

Hell were sundered. With Satan's followers began the eternal restlessness that is the result of imperfection striving to regain, or attain, perfection. The association between lack of rest and loss of virtue can be found in *Comus,* where Milton says of evil,

> It shall be in eternal restless change
> Self-fed and self-consum'd. (596–97)

Change enters a changeless universe only with sin, i.e., imperfection in action. The lost, homeless state of man came to seem his peculiar curse, and Milton's lines on the wandering angels are confirmed in "The Pulley" and "Man" by his contemporaries George Herbert and Henry Vaughan.

At two places in Book I the total meaning of *rest* for Milton's design emerges clearly. There is the melancholy, sighing rhythm of a few lines when we first see Hell:

> Regions of sorrow, doleful shades, where peace
> And rest can never dwell, hope never comes
> That comes to all. (i.65–67)

The poignancy is in the repeated *never,* for this negative of the happy eternity of Heaven was unknown until this moment. The elliptical phrase, "that comes to all," is there to remind us of the essential *difference* between ourselves and the fallen angels, which is brought out more strongly at the end of the poem; our struggles do have an end in rest, while theirs last eternally. The angel Abdiel, in his exchange with Satan, predicts a dateless future:

> Apostat, still thou errst, nor end wilt find
> Of erring, from the path of truth remote. (vi.172–73)

The *likeness* between the sin of men and of angels, on the other hand, is emphasized in another appearance of *never,* with a still more threatening undertone, just before Eve meets the serpent; again, the idea of rest accompanies it.

> Thou never from that houre in Paradise
> Foundst either sweet repast, or sound repose. (ix.406–7)

Rest makes its second important appearance in Book I in a parenthetical remark of Satan as he urges his followers toward the "dreary Plain":

> Thither let us tend
> From off the tossing of these fiery waves,
> There rest, if any rest can harbour there. (i.183–85)

Milton's verb, *harbour,* strengthens the suggestion of the quest for security and calm by making the angels mariners seeking a haven from a stormy ocean. Later, the idea of "no rest" for the weary is allegorized in the incessantly barking offspring of Sin, who complains, "Rest or intermission none I find" (ii.802). The antithesis of the harassments in Hell is found in Eden as Adam leads Eve to the bower:

> Fair Consort, th' hour
> Of night, and all things now retir'd to rest
> Mind us of like repose, since God hath set
> Labour and rest, as day and night to men
> Successive. (iv.610–14)

The idea is several times repeated in Milton's account of Paradise; and at the Creation itself, a kind of cosmic rest emerges from restless Chaos. Raphael begins his account with a picture of the achieved, "poised" stillness of the quiet earth itself:

> As yet this world was not, and *Chaos* wilde
> Reignd where these Heav'ns now rowl, where Earth now rests
> Upon her Center pois'd. (v.577–79)

The tremor of restlessness re-enters, however, with Satan,

who is warned by Michael, "think not here To trouble Holy Rest" (vi.271–72). Satan's intention is exactly that, nevertheless; he has first "disturb'd Heav'ns blessed peace" (vi.266–67), and now turns to trouble the rest of the Garden. The unquiet of evil is manifest in its disregard for the orderly cycles of rest and waking that are the basis of health in living things; hostile to life, it seeks to destroy the processes by which life maintains itself. An earlier example of this intent, not quite so explicit, is found in Comus, who appears at sunset to ask, "What hath night to do with sleep?" (122). Satan's temptation in Eve's dream follows the same line — "Why sleepst thou *Eve?*" Night, moon, and stars prevail,

> in vain,
> If none regard; Heav'n wakes with all his eyes,
> Whom to behold but thee, Natures desire . . . (v.43–45)

The angels who come to foil his designs observe that he is "imploi'd it seems to violate sleep" (iv.883) — the very original of Comus.

After the first day's battle in Heaven, the rebels withdraw, already fatally afflicted.

> *Satan* with his rebellious disappeerd,
> Far in the dark dislodg'd, and void of rest. (vi.414–15)

So, after the Fall, we find Adam and Eve:

> thir shame in part
> Coverd, but not at rest or ease of Mind,
> They sate them down to weep. (ix.1119–20)

The end sought in vain by the fallen angels is given to man, however, and with it his place of rest. We suffer,

> till we end
> In dust, our final rest and native home. (x.1084–85)

The last variation on this theme comes in a passage from the
final book. In it, Milton ties up neatly several threads of diction and imagery; it illustrates the nature of the journey and
its goal. Jesus will quell

> The adversarie Serpent, and bring back
> Through the worlds wilderness long wanderd man
> Safe to eternal Paradise of rest. (xii.312–14)

Every word is significantly connected with the mythological
themes of the poem. "Bring back" suggests the circular
journey; *wilderness,* with its reminiscence of the forest and
the maze, along with *safe,* indicate its danger. *Long* brings in
the temporal dimension necessary to this part of the myth.
And in the last phrase, the time-ridden win eternity, the out-
casts Eden, the tired wanderers rest.

   The word *wander* has almost always a pejorative, or melancholy, connotation in *Paradise Lost.* It is a key word, summarizing the theme of the erring, bewildered human pilgrimage,
and its extension into the prelapsarian world with the
fallen angels. As pagan gods, they are seen "wandring ore
the Earth" (i.365); in Hell after Satan's departure, they "dis-
band, and wandring, each his several way Pursues"
(ii.523–24), or becomes lost in philosophic mazes. The theme
here meshes with a closely allied though minor image, a
persistent favorite with Milton, the labyrinth. It stands
for the difficulties of the dark voyage, the stage where the
monster is encountered and the deceitful sorcerer appears
with "baits and seeming pleasures." In *Comus,* the "Sun-
clad power of Chastity" shines forth even from the labyrin-
thine "huge Forrests, and unharbour'd Heaths";

> Yea there, where very desolation dwels
> By grots, and caverns shag'd with horrid shades,
> She may pass on with unblench't majesty. (428–30)

Almost all the images of danger that surround the journey of life are here: forest, desert, hills, caves. Later, Milton used the image in prose, emphasizing the difference between the straightness of heaven and the dangerous crookedness of earth: "the ways of the Lord straight and faithful as they are, not full of cranks and contradictions, and pitfalling dispenses." [4] But the most dangerous labyrinth is in the human soul, "the wily subtleties and refluxes of man's thoughts." [5] Mazes, crooked ways, labyrinths, and "refluxes," are all to be found on a larger scale in *Paradise Lost;* they indicate the wayward and misleading powers of error, of which the serpent himself is the physical embodiment.

> Lead then, said *Eve.* Hee leading swiftly rowld
> In tangles, and made intricate seem strait,
> To mischief swift. Hope elevates, and joy
> Bright'ns his Crest, as when a wandring Fire
> Compact of unctuous vapor, which the Night
> Condenses, and the cold invirons round,
> Which oft, they say, some evil Spirit attends,
> Hovering and blazing with delusive Light,
> Misleads th' amaz'd Night-wanderer from his way.
>   (ix.631–40)

The intrusion of cold and night into a pastoral scene of "blowing Myrrh and Balme" casts a sudden chill over Eden, and the intricate tangles of the serpent, the wandering course, hark back to the "brazen foulds" of the gate in Pandemonium (i.724) and the "scaly fould" of Sin (ii.651); the passage also looks ahead to Adam's perplexity after the Fall.

> All my evasions vain
> And reasonings, though through Mazes, lead me still
> But to my own conviction. (x.829–31)

[4] *Doctrine and Discipline, SM,* p. 576.
[5] *Reason of Church Government, SM,* p. 525.

Not only moral values, but the intellectual values on which they depend, can be objectified in Milton's topography, by the identification of physical and spiritual "wandering." *Error* is the linking word. The Paradise of Fools, "o're the backside of the World," includes follies that are defined as errors in the physical sense — wanderings off course, mistaking one place for another.

> Here Pilgrims roam, that stray'd so farr to seek
> In *Golgotha* him dead, who lives in Heav'n. (iii.476–77)

There is, too, the errant Satan, "from the path of truth remote," and his complement, Abdiel, who refuses to "swerve from truth" (v.902). Adam foresees an endless happiness, remote from "all anxious care" and confusion,

> unless we our selves
> Seek them with wandring thoughts, and notions vaine.
> But apte the Mind or Fancie is to roave
> Uncheckt, and of her roaving is no end. (viii.186–89)

In the end, despite his momentary wisdom, he is the victim of "wandring vanitie" (x.875). Milton carries the same images and diction into *Samson Agonistes* to indicate the doubt and perplexity from which Samson's ancestor, Adam, had prayed to be delivered, and to which his contemporaries had fallen prey, who

> give the rains to wandring thought,
> Regardless of his glories diminution;
> Till by thir own perplexities involv'd
> They ravel more, still less resolv'd,
> But never find self-satisfying solution. (300–309)

These wanderers are the lineal descendants of the angels in Hell who found themselves lost in wandering mazes.

The most memorable instance of Milton's use of *wander* is the phrase "wandring steps and slow" at the close of *Paradise Lost;* almost equally suggestive is Eve's speech as the recognition of her loss becomes part of her consciousness.

> From thee
> How shall I part, and whither wander down
> Into a lower World, to this obscure
> And wilde, how shall we breath in other Aire
> Less pure, accustomed to immortal Fruits? (xi.281–85)

Milton's adjectives call on the archetypes already established in the major action, to characterize the new, strange world: *obscure,* because farther removed from the fountain of light, and because the planets that illuminate it have been turned oblique; *wilde,* because nature is now hostile; its air *less pure* than the clear brilliance of Paradise.

The lesser perplexities and wanderings of *Paradise Lost* are anticipations or echoes of Satan's flight to earth; in Francis Fergusson's phrase, they are "analogous actions," with Satan the ultimate analogue. His voyage, in turn, reinforces the parallel between the two falls. In the nature of Satan's journey we can find, perhaps, one of the sources of our sympathy, or empathy, with him — a sympathy that has been excused, applauded, justified, and denied, but will never be explained to everyone's satisfaction. Some of Milton's most intimate feelings were certainly involved in his portrait of Satan, but the nature of those feelings may have been more universal than his rebellious Puritan independence. Satan's pilgrimage through the dark toward Paradise re-traces the necessity that life imposes on us all. His cry, "Long is the way and hard, that out of Hell leads up to light," speaks to an emotion almost universal, the same that answers Dante's verses —

salimmo suso, ei primo ed io secondo,
tanto ch' io vidi delle cose belle
che porta il ciel, per un pertugio tondo;

e quindi uscimmo a riverder le stelle.[6]

The urge to regain "the Archetype of the Vanishing Garden" "draws sustenance from the unplumbed depths of our individual and collective unconscious." [7] Satan, exiled from Heaven, seeks compensation in man's Garden for his lost glory, tracing in the process the first of many quests.

The idea of Satan as outcast and wanderer was, of course, traditional, and evidently appealed to Milton from the beginning. In his youthful poem, *In quintum Novembris*, the Devil is described as "aethero vagus exul Olympo." We can see a faint shadow of a more distant voyage in his circling of the globe, and in his journey to Rome the ghost of his primordial quest.

Hactenus; & piceis liquido natat aere pennis;
Qua volat, adversi praecursant agmine venti,
Densantur nubes, & crebra tonitrua fulgent.
    Iamque pruinosas velox superaverat alpes,
Et tenet Ausoniae fines.[8]

Milton's lines call to mind another seeker of the Ausonian

---

[6] "We mounted up, he first and I second, so far that I distinguished through a round opening the beauteous things which Heaven bears; and thence we issued out, again to see the Stars." *Inferno*, xxiv.136–139. Translated by John Aitken Carlyle. The Temple Classics (London, 1941), pp. 390–91.

[7] Philip Wheelwright, "Notes on Mythopoeia," *Sewanee Review*, LIX (1951), 589.

[8] "This and no more; then with his pitch-black wings he swims in the liquid air. Wherever he flies, warring winds in battalions race before him, the clouds thicken, and the thunder and lightning are incessant.

"And now he had swiftly passed over the ice-mantled Alps and was within the borders of Ausonia." *In quintum Novembris*, ll. 45–59. Translated by N. G. McCrea.

land, in whose story was embedded the mythological theme
of a journey toward a promised land.

> Vivite felices, quibus est fortuna peracta
> iam sua; nos alia ex aliis in fata vocamur.
> Vobis parta quies; nullum maris aequor arandum
> arva neque Ausoniae semper cedentia retro
> quaerenda.[9]

Whether it is the vanishing garden or the ever-vanishing
Ausonian shore, the object of the quest is really the same:
a home, a haven, safety, rest; or, if one likes, "the womb's
security."

The voyage of Books II and III is Milton's greatest "original" creation. There was precedent for the journey motif
in epic tradition, but no real parallel to a voyage by Satan in
the Christian literature on which Milton drew. The germ of
the theme may have been suggested by Grotius' *Adamus
Exul*, which opens with "Sathan" proclaiming his intentions
in soliloquy.

> Hac spe, per omnes Orbis ibo terminos,
> Hac spe citatus, clausa littoribus vagis
> Transibo maria, saevus ut rictu Leo
> Patulo timendus per locorum devia
> Quaerit quod avido dente dilaniet pecus.[10]

---

[9] "Fare ye well, ye whose own destiny is already achieved; we are still sum-
moned from fate to fate. Your rest is won. No ocean plains need ye plough,
no ever-retreating Ausonian fields need ye seek." *Aeneid* iii.493–97.
Translated by H. Rushton Fairclough. *Virgil*, I, 380–81.

[10] "In this hope, I shall go through all the Globe's wide bounds;
  Spurr'd by this hope I'll cross the seas, hemm'd in
  By wandering shores; just as a cruel lion seeks
  Through wandering ways, with formidable open jaws,
  Some hapless flock that he may rend with greedy fangs."
Translated by Watson Kirkonnell. *The Celestial Cycle* (Toronto, 1952), pp.
98–99.

There were, too, contemporary "influences" at work on Milton, as Marjorie Nicolson has reminded us. "Satan's voyage through Chaos is one of the great 'cosmic voyages' of a period that sent imaginary mariners to the moon and planets in search of other worlds and other men." [11] Milton's conception of Satan's journey remains unique, however, and more powerfully suggestive than any comparable treatment.

Complexity and suggestiveness enter at the start when we consider Chaos, the primordial ocean. Satan's traverse of it is an attempt to heal his impaired perfection, whether that be interpreted psychologically as a defeat by "the archaic forces of the unconscious," or morally as a fall into the disorder of sin which, Milton once wrote, is "as boundless as that vacuity beyond the world." [12] Satan is, of course, going about the repair in the wrong way; he supposes that the achievement of Paradise or "some milde Zone" will divest him of gloom and anguish, not realizing that with his loss of Heaven he has also lost the sympathy with outward things that will allow them to touch and influence him. The nature of his quest and its failure are both indicated in an observation by Milton as Satan, entering the Garden, perches on the Tree of Life, "like a Cormorant."

> Yet not true Life
> Thereby regaind, but sat devising Death
> To them who liv'd; nor on the vertue thought
> Of that life-giving Plant, but only us'd
> For prospect, what well us'd had bin the pledge
> Of immortalitie. (iv.196–201)

Satan has been seeking a return to the immortal life he lost; and Milton includes in these lines a hint to more fortunate pilgrims that God's gifts, "well us'd," *can* lead to Para-

---

[11] *The Breaking of the Circle* (Evanston, Illinois, 1950), p. 165.
[12] *Tetrachordon, SM*, p. 684.

dise regained. Unregenerate, Satan brings his Hell with him.

His mission is, nevertheless, the traditional one of the hero, who seeks to renew or restore the kingdom for his people by winning some "treasure hard to attain." The images accord, therefore, with traditional accounts of the quest; the two basic ones, sea (Chaos) and pilgrimage, are really inseparable. Satan's role as pilgrim requires the dolorous regions through which he will pass. In accordance with epic precedent, the journey is expressed quite consistently in the imagery of a voyage, though the desert and wooded wilderness, also suitable quest-scenes, are never far away. Satan's first proposal of the search for Paradise, in the council of Hell, is like the previews in fairy tales, legend, and romance, of the perilous quest to be undertaken by the knight.

> What strength, what art can then
> Suffice, or what evasion bear him safe
> Through the strict Senteries and Stations thick
> Of Angels watching round? (ii.410–13)

A similar prospect confronts the Red Cross Knight setting out through the Wood of Error for the redemption of a symbolic city hedged about with perils, though his chief peril is not an angel, but a reincarnation of the old Serpent himself, who has changed his role to that of challenger. Another analogue is the hero of the *Romance of the Rose* attempting to enter a garden defended by allegorical sentries. The path to be followed by them all is "the Road of Trials," "a dream landscape of curiously fluid, ambiguous forms"; [13] it is the "dim domain that has been for milleniums the holy goal of all the great questing heroes, from Gilgamesh to Faust." [14]

---

[13] Campbell, *Hero with a Thousand Faces,* p. 97.

[14] Heinrich Zimmer, *The King and the Corpse,* ed. Joseph Campbell (New York, 1947), p. 84.

As the final quotation suggests, the later heroes of myth usually reversed Satan's path, their first "holy goal" being the realm of death, from whose perils they returned to gain their reward in the shape of regained Paradise. Satan has ventured down, too, but his descent was involuntary. And his reascending quest is motivated by destructive rather than constructive impulses; though he starts out to seek a place where he can heal the scars of Hell, or reintegrate his personality, he ends by wanting merely to destroy the place, and his final fall is a further ignominious disintegration. Satan fails, as he must always fail; but his inverted image, with a successful end, is the pilgrim of *The Divine Comedy*. Our hopes and fears may not extend as high as Dante's or as low as Satan's, but we are bound on the same route. For man, the object of God's mercy as well as his wrath, trial may be "that which purifies us." But it is still a trial: "the way seems difficult and steep to scale" (ii.71).

Satan anticipates the trials awaiting him, in his speech accepting "alone the dreadful voyage." There is the void of Night, in which he will be threatened with "utter loss of being" — the descent into a pre-personal world where selfhood is swallowed up in the "abortive gulf" of unconscious and racial memory. There follows the journey through the unknown land.

> If thence he scape into what ever world,
> Or unknown Region, what remains him less
> Then unknown dangers and as hard escape. (ii.442–44)

After all, Satan's voyage is very like traditional "descents," even though he starts from deep Hell and not, like earthly heroes, from the light of day. In his speech to his angels, he makes Hell seem almost a haven, compared to the dangers awaiting him outside, and his entry into Chaos is as devastating as a true descent to the underworld. The grim guardians of Hell Gate are the first of his obstacles, and in his encounter with them we can see clearly for the first time Milton's design for his voyage. Once Satan has been allowed by God to escape from Hell, there is really no reason why he should not be immediately transferred to Paradise, where the main action of the Fall will begin. No reason, that is, *except* Milton's intention of including the great archetype of the journey in his poem. To be faithful to it, he had to include the trials of traditional quest-literature, and so Sin, Death, and the kingdom of Chaos are stationed in Satan's path. Like other heroes, he finds monsters in the Deep. Sin, with her scaly folds, is a combination of the old serpent of the ocean and another dream-figure, the siren or lamia, "who infatuates the lonely wanderer"; Milton's description of her accords with old illustrations of lamias, as well as with verbal accounts.[15] Northrop Frye has said that the "darkness, winter and dissolution phase" of the universal myth contains as two of its standard subordinate characters "the ogre and the witch"; [16] they, too, probably find ancestors in Milton's Sin and Death.

It is interesting, too, that allegorical beings, whose introduction into *Paradise Lost* has distracted so many critics, should inhabit the section of the poem that contains the favorite theme of allegory. Satan, a fallen creature, is already beginning to live in a world of allegorical symbols instead of myth. There is a family resemblance between Milton's Sin and Death and the traditional personages of allegory to whom they stand as grandparents, and the similarity has tended to obscure their place in *Paradise Lost*.

---

[15] See Jung, *Psychology and Alchemy*, p. 52, for comments on this creature, with old illustrations.

[16] "The Archetypes of Literature," *Kenyon Review*, XIII (1951), 105.

Johnson, who considered "this unskilful allegory . . . one of the greatest faults of the poem," recognized, though he did not applaud, the *un*traditional character of Milton's figures.

To exalt causes into agents, to invest abstract ideas with form, and animate them with activity has always been the right of poetry. But such airy beings are for the most part suffered only to do their natural office, and retire. Thus Fame tells a tale and Victory hovers over a general or perches on a standard; but Fame and Victory can do no more. To give them any real employment or ascribe to them any material agency is to make them allegorical no longer, but to shock the mind by ascribing effects to non-entity.[17]

Johnson's idea of allegory was, indeed, more circumscribed than it should have been; but more liberal standards cannot quite accommodate Milton's Sin under the conventional label of allegory, either. She is larger and more solid even than most of Bunyan's characters, the very incarnation of whatever is horrible and fascinating in evil. In the total context of *Paradise Lost,* she and Death are, as Johnson said, "allegorical no longer," but it is because Milton's "abstractions" are always substances, not because they are nonentities. When we first encounter them, with Satan, they call up so many echoes of others of their species that we seem to be already in a familiar world of disembodied abstractions. Later, however, when they enter the fallen world, we can see that they represent the last stage of Milton's *mythical* presentation. He had promised to tell how the Fall "brought Death into the World" and, since the story in its main outlines was mythical, the invasion of earth's frail shell by a literal, concrete Death was necessary, as had been the literal

---

17 *Lives of the Poets,* I, 185. Interestingly, Johnson also objects to Force and Victory in that very "mythological" play, *Prometheus Bound.*

birth of Sin from Satan described in Book II. Once the
Fall has taken place, the myth recedes into memory, to be
replaced by new modes of experience, and it is at the point
where it begins to recede that Sin and Death build their
bridge. These two creatures live on the borderline between
myth and allegory, between a world where physical and
spiritual forces are identical, and a world where spiritual
force is merely indicated by physical. They are neither
wholly mythic nor completely allegorical. Sin can already
separate her body from her power, because the quality embodied in her has been shattered by man's sin and distributed through the many bodies of the mortally stricken universe.

> Mean while in Paradise the hellish pair
> Too soon arriv'd, *Sin* there in power before,
> Once actual, now in body, and to dwell
> Habitual habitant. (x.585–88)

With Eve's sin (that is, when, with a sinful act, Sin became
"actual"), a part of the archetype is separated from itself,
and the fragment lodged in the human soul. Henceforth,
because sin will be so widespread, no single representation
of her can be complete; Milton's is the last full-length portrait before the destruction of archetypes.[18]

The whole of Book X, indeed, hovers on the threshold
between literal and figurative, and it is impossible to accept
the bridge from Hell quite as unreservedly as "real," as the
cosmography of Book III. This change seems to be reflected
even in the style; the description of the bridge-building has

---

[18] In the Kingdom of Chaos, Milton also placed Night, Rumour, Chance,
and such representatives of confusion as Discord. They are appropriate enough
in the mixed, indeterminate world of Chaos; but may be, after all, only
vestiges of older conceptions like those recorded in the Cambridge Manuscript.

struck many readers as odd, and is in fact much more particular and specialized than Milton's ordinary mythical language. Mr. Empson objects to the passage about "Gorgonian rigor" on the ground that it "shows the process of finding concrete for abstract caught half-way"; [19] this is an exact account of what is really happening at that moment in the world of the poem, and Milton's style can be justified by saying that he was reproducing in it the half-real, half-imaginary quality of his subject.

Though their ontological status is ambiguous, Sin and Death, by their presence in Book II, help us to translate Satan's voyage into the terms of more familiar earthly pilgrimages. The process is assisted by Milton's allusions; a collection of famous voyagers make the voyaging Satan recognizable. Sin becomes an Homeric monster:

> Far less abhorrd then these
> Vex'd *Scylla* bathing in the Sea that parts
> *Calabria* from the hoarce *Trinacrian* shore. (ii.659–61)

Far into Chaos, Satan is beset by warring elements; he is, once more, Odysseus, and also Jason:

> Harder beset
> And more endanger'd, then when *Argo* pass'd
> Through *Bosporus* betwixt the justling Rocks:
> Or when *Ulysses* on the Larbord shunnd
> *Charybdis,* and by th' other whirlpool steard. (ii.1016–20)

He has already likened earth to "the happy Ile" (ii.410); the association is made again as he approaches Eden.

> Or other Worlds they seemd, or happy Iles,
> Like those *Hesperian* Gardens fam'd of old. (iii.567–68)

19 *Some Versions of Pastoral*, p. 154.

Earth is one Paradise among the starry Islands of the Blest that were the objects of nostalgia for the classical world. Their number and beauty gives a sense of almost dizzying opulence, as though Satan were swimming in the very atmosphere of a dream-paradise. As islands, the stars reinforce the image of the voyage; as Paradise, they support its spiritual intention.

Sometimes the inspiration for the imagery of these books comes not from other myths, but from the excitement of an opening world that had pricked the imaginations of poets for a century or more. Milton's geographical interests find ample scope in Satan's voyage along the unknown "coasts of dark destruction." The flagship for which Satan's spear in Book I provided a mast taller than the tallest Norwegian pine, becomes a whole fleet as he launches into Chaos, in the simile of the merchants on the "Trading Flood" (ii.636 ff.). By the time he comes in sight of the new world, he is weather-beaten, "glad that now his Sea should find a shore" (ii.1011), however brief his sojourn there.

> *Satan* with less toil, and now with ease
> Wafts on the calmer wave by dubious light
> And like a weather-beaten Vessel holds
> Gladly the Port, though Shrouds and Tackle torn. (ii.1041–44)

In the last lines of Book II, the voice of Milton speaks through the imagery to characterize this vessel; it is "full fraught with mischievous revenge" (ii.1054). Finally, as he is about to enter the Garden, Satan is a wolf and a thief, but he is also the mariner off the Cape of Good Hope, cheered by the grateful smell of Araby the Blest (iv.159 ff.).

Just as significant mythologically are the passages in which Satan's voyage is transported to land, and the theme is carried by images of the quest in the desert.

> Wandring this darksome Desart, as my way
> Lies through your spacious Empire up to light,
> Alone, and without guide, half lost, I seek
> What readiest path . . . (ii.973–76)

The major image of Book III is of Satan as a wilderness wanderer.

>   As when a Scout
> Through dark and desert wayes with peril gone
> All night; at last by break of chearful dawne
> Obtains the brow of some high-climbing Hill . . . (iii.543–46)

After Book IV, the quest images cease, to resume after the Fall when man, too, has become a wanderer. There is a last allusion to Satan as a "great adventurer" awaited by his host (x.440); and Milton did not finally abandon the image until he had used it of the Satan of *Paradise Regained*. The Devil is still fruitlessly wandering the earth, finding no end; the "eternal restless change" of evil is incarnate in him, forcing from him a final despairing cry:

> I would be at my worst; worst is my Port,
> My harbour and my ultimate repose,
> The end I would attain, my final good. (iii.209–11)

Paradise Regained is an "answer" to *Paradise Lost* in several ways; the answer is stated mythically in the "wilderness" imagery that makes Christ an instance of the hero beset by dangers. It is clear that Milton intended his Christ, wandering a "pathless Desert, dusk with horrid shades" (*P.R.*, i.296), to be the counterweight to Satan in *Paradise Lost,* also a pilgrim, but an erring one. Together they enact man's fate. An appropriate, if temporary, close is achieved in the last line of *Paradise Regained,* where Jesus is brought "home to his

Mothers house"; the house is an ancient and natural enough emblem for the goal, resting-place, or harbor sought by the traveler. The most profound parallel between Satan and Christ, Milton did not choose to depict in his poetry; but the descent of the Savior to the lower regions is alluded to in traditional mythological terms in the *Christian Doctrine*.

> Hence it appears that baptism was intended to represent figuratively the painful life of Christ, his death and burial, in which he was immersed, as it were, for a season.[20]

The waters of death received Christ, as the "waters" of Chaos had received Satan.

Into the adventures and exploits of Satan in the first four books of *Paradise Lost,* Milton incorporated not only explicit images of voyaging and pilgrimage, but also a number of motifs familiar to us in the literature of our own perplexed lives. Satan encounters and experiences, in anticipation or simile, the sinful world he is to create; indeed, we see him creating it as he goes along. After the colloquy with Sin and Death, with its forecast of "Pestilence and Warr" (ii.711), he comes upon the Anarch, Chaos, and "Sable-vested Night, eldest of things," whose arrival on earth will make the good things of day begin to droop and drowse and force a prayer from the benighted traveler; witness the Elder Brother of *Comus,* invoking moon and stars:

> Stoop thy pale visage through an amber cloud,
> And disinherit *Chaos,* that raigns here
> In double night of darkness and of shades. (733-35)

The episode of the Paradise of Fools and its procession of future human trumpery is similarly prophetic. Satan also

---

[20] I, xxviii. *SM,* p. 1031.

wears many of the guises he is to put on in the world's legends; he is, almost from the start of the voyage, the "specious object" against whom Eve is warned (ix.361). In his meeting with Uriel, he is the transformed wizard, ancestor of Archimago and Duessa — "the first That practisd falshood under saintly shew" (iv.121–22). Here he is a cherub; elsewhere a "Vultur on *Imaus* bred . . . to gorge the flesh of Lambs" (iii.431–34); shapeshifted again, a toad; and once more, "a Lion now he stalkes with fierie glare, Then as a Tyger," anticipating the hostile environment where beasts will threaten "gentle Fawnes at play" (iv.402–4). The mount of Paradise, assaulted by this "prowling Wolfe," suggests all the other enclosed treasures destined to fall prey to Satan's descendants. The accumulation of references to our familiar delusions and perils — the will-o'-the-wisp and Leviathan are others, placed elsewhere in the poem — shows once more the usefulness to Milton's scheme of the Satan sub-plot, in drawing into the mythical "present" of the poem the "future" of legend and history.

In the middle books of *Paradise Lost,* Milton is occupied with the still, changeless image of Paradise, and with the War, first on the soil of Heaven, then in the soul of man. Books IV through VIII are a still center of his turning world; Satan's quest leads up to them, and man's quest — both for the Paradise within, and for the lost Garden itself — leads away, down into the lower world of Biblical history. Dryden was perhaps the first to notice the modulation at the close of *Paradise Lost* into the symbolism of *The Faerie Queene* and its peers. He would have ranked Milton higher, he said, "if the giant had not foiled the knight, and driven him out of his stronghold, to wander through the world with his lady errant." [21] This was a fanciful way of stating his

21 *Essays of John Dryden,* ed. W. P. Ker (2 vols., Oxford, 1900), II, 165.

objection to the "unhappy" ending of *Paradise Lost;* but the observation itself is accurate, and we may see a special virtue in the integration of the great Christian myth with the most universal of mythological themes. Dryden's statement indicates the ease with which the *dénouement* of *Paradise Lost* can be translated into the familiar terms of courtly romance, and thence into the allegory of Everyman. Tillyard has developed the idea in his remark that, at the end of the poem, Milton "in the manner of Spenser" presents Adam and Eve as "Everyman and Everywoman . . . setting out on their earthly quest for a mental paradise." [22]

Milton dovetails his two journeys — the proto-human and the human — in a pointed line as Satan achieves, for the moment, his goal: "His journies end and our beginning woe" (iii.633). Time, in the consciousness of the first fallen creature, has led up to this moment, and time and struggle, the keynotes of fallen human consciousness, will follow. The transference of the quest theme from Satan to man is made plain later in the poem's action, but it is epitomized in this line. The nature of the "beginning woe," the life journey, is shown in the prophecy of Book III, where the shift of the pilgrim's progress to man's soul is described by God:

> And I will place within them as a guide
> My Umpire *Conscience,* whom if they will hear,
> Light after light well us'd they shall attain,
> And to the end persisting, safe arrive. (iii.194–97)

This reads almost like a summary of Christian's safe arrival at the Heavenly City; it is echoed in the final book —

> Through the worlds wilderness long wanderd man
> Safe to eternal Paradise of rest. (xii.313–14)

22 *Miltonic Setting,* pp. 202–3.

The quests of the Old Testament have, by this time, provided concrete examples of mankind's characteristic fate; the last books are full of journeys. Adam's phrase for Noah suggests again "the worlds wilderness": the patriarch is seen "wandring that watrie Desert" (xi.779), the prototype of later travelers for whom Milton had once invoked the aid of Lycidas — "all that wander in that perilous flood." The endless Biblical pilgrimages related by Michael include Moses leading the Israelites, and Abraham,

Not wandring poor, but trusting all his wealth
With God, who call'd him, in a land unknown. (xii.133–34)

All these, taken together, telescope the theme of the life journey, which is to be continued through the generations until "long wanderd man" is brought safely home.

The two most striking "interludes" in the main structure of *Paradise Lost* are both essential to the success of Milton's epic as a mythological poem. The introduction, at the beginning, of Satan's voyage, and at the end, of history seen in panorama, spatially rather than temporally, allow him to include the second major area of the Christian myth in his "architectural" plan. They give us a vision of human history in a form that is non-historical. The life of man is encompassed within the very walls of the City of God, on which Milton founded his changeless, eternal structure.

CONCLUSION

To describe the meaning of a work of art completely is impossible, since the meaning is articulated only in the finished work itself. The best summary of a critical analysis is a re-reading of the work analyzed, so that the coarse discriminations of criticism may be replaced by the finer ones of art. Our first experience in reading a poem or a novel is a unified one; our final experience should be the same. The complexity of *Paradise Lost* is visible to anyone who has penetrated even slightly beneath the surface. What should be just as visible, but often is not, is its enormous simplicity. A myth seeks to circumscribe, depict, explain basic realities of human experience; and, in the end, the facts that we can call basic are few. Only they are hard to disinter from the welter of irrelevance and triviality that surrounds each of our lives. Milton's poem is, perhaps, most truly mythological in its comprehensiveness, in the boldness and breadth of its outlines, the relevance of its design to the fundamental issues of the soul's life. The images of *Paradise Lost* knit us, even in an urban and scientific age, to the world around us and to each other. They are the polar elements that go to compose our mixed unity and the systole and diastole that we observe in nature. Joined to the rhythmic alternation of opposites in *Paradise Lost,* as we have seen, is another pattern, almost as ancient: the threefold mythical scheme of loss, quest, and return.

The themes contained in these images — vast, resonant, living at the roots of human life — were perfectly congenial to Milton's genius. "No theme and no setting, other than that which he chose in *Paradise Lost,* could have given him such scope for the kind of imagery in which he excelled"; [1] and, conversely, no other imagery could have expressed so completely the themes that had always compelled his imagination. If any poet ever *thought* in terms of myth, Milton did. Having said this, however, one must move on to qualifications. The myth, in the poem, has been assimilated into a larger design, which cannot be called mythical in any sense acceptable to modern theory; it becomes part of a moral pattern that is actually anti-mythical. In the course of this transformation, it has moved away from its early development in "primitive" or pre-Christian minds. It is to be ordered into a scale of values; to be turned into a religion, made to accommodate a theology.

One of the essential qualities of myth, in its original state, is its shiftiness. The personages and images of mythology are fluid, their meaning often ambiguous. The unity of the mythical world enforced a basic instability.

The limits between the different spheres are not insurmountable barriers; they are fluent and fluctuating. There is no specific difference between the various realms of life. Nothing has a definite, invariable, static shape. By a sudden metamorphosis everything may be turned into everything. If there is any characteristic and outstanding feature of the mythical world, any law by which it is governed — it is this law of metamorphosis.[2]

It is hard to think of a paragraph that would be less pertinent to Milton's world in *Paradise Lost.* For, as Blake said,

---

1 Eliot, "Milton," *Sewanee Review,* LVI (1948), 198.
2 Cassirer, *Essay on Man,* p. 81.

"In Eternity one Thing never Changes into another Thing. Each Identity is Eternal." [3] The myth of Milton's eternity is the product of a sensibility civilized, rational, and above all, moral. Held in the perspective of good and evil, these eternal identities take on clearer outlines; they have a definite, bounded quality unknown to their earliest incarnations. Milton's life was ruled by the conviction that moral choice, and the distinctions on which it is based, are not only possible but necessary. Freud has said that dreams — "the myths of the individual" — are characterized by "an absence of either-or." [4] The fluid boundaries of primitive myth do not lend themselves to the clear presentation of moral issues, where either-or is demanded, and they must therefore be fixed by a stiffening process either moral or aesthetic, or both.

From this it follows that myth, for Milton, was what we have seen it to be in examining *Paradise Lost:* a structural and epistemological principle, reflecting accurately, as he thought, the real nature of our first world. It was never, in itself, a moral principle, so that in the process of accommodating Milton's moral intuitions, it loses some of the qualities technically belonging to myth, in particular its magical, shape-shifting versatility. Milton was willing to admit that ambiguity exists; he would have agreed that good and evil may spring from the same root, that right and wrong are two directions confronting one force in the soul. The intimate union of opposed qualities in a single organism is necessary for life, as the Garden of *Paradise Lost* attests. Even in Hell, we see the distorted outlines of something heavenly, and Satan the ruined leader was "brighter once

---

[3] *Vision of the Last Judgment, Poetry and Prose*, p. 640.
[4] *Wit and Its Relation to the Unconscious, The Basic Writings of Sigmund Freud*, ed. A. A. Brill, The Modern Library (New York, 1938), p. 780.

amidst the Host Of Angels" than the brightest star (vii. 132–33). Milton's picture of Chaos is the best evidence that he recognized genuine ambiguity when he saw it, and did not flinch from it. Chaos is tormented by real ambivalence, because it is still potential; "*Chance* governs all" because no end has been appointed to any of the warring elements. With the emergence of actuality striving toward an end, chance ceases to operate, and fulfilment in the ordained shape, or deviation from it, ensues. All things come of Chaos, perhaps; but once they have come, they are no longer the same. Milton never committed the genetic fallacy which claims that good and evil are rendered indistinguishable when they are seen to have a common source. They are often hard to distinguish, but it is our duty to do so.

In reading *Paradise Lost,* then, we have a sense at once of completeness and of limitation, and this is as Milton would have wished. The completeness comes from the poem's capacity to surround human life, so that every point on the circumference of our days is touched — even though, as Virginia Woolf thought, the private selfhood at the center may remain untouched, darkly unregarded. The limitation comes from Milton's insistence on portraying his mythical images as embodiments of definite moral qualities. The spirit that sees the denial of limit as the only path to full humanity will condemn the fixed boundaries of *Paradise Lost* as a crippling fault. Limit can also be regarded, however, as the condition of any complete individuality, in man or poem. "Nothing is complete which has no end," Aristotle observed; "and the end is a limit." [5] Whether *end* is taken as a physical boundary or as *telos,* the implication is the same: completeness, by its very nature, involves limitation; to be

[5] *Physics,* 207a, trans. R. P. Hardie and R. K. Gaye, *The Basic Works of Aristotle,* ed. Richard McKeon (New York, 1951), p. 267.

thus is *not* to be otherwise. A systematic view of life is complete only when it has imposed certain defining boundaries. Belief in system and limit is part of a major strain in European thought, though it is a view alien to our own anarchic, confused society, where every creature is rootless or incomplete, by definition or desire. Milton's classicism is not a mere matter of allusions and similes; in the assertion of limit, he is most deeply classical. At the same time, he is most truly Christian, for human limitation is a corollary to the belief in a single infinity, God.

It is one of the axioms of modern "psychological" mythology that myths exist to show the way, through the example of the hero, to a full integration of the personality. Jung insists on the necessity of including opposites in any complete view of life, of exploring all four compass points, recognizing all four "faculties" in the psyche. The persistent theme of the night journey indicates that if we are to be whole, we must descend into the darkest places of the soul; completeness is hard-won.

Before he can cope with the multiplicity of life's forces, he must be introduced to the universal law of coexisting opposites. . . . For he does not yet understand that the pattern of existence is woven of antagonistic co-operation, alternations of ascendancy and decline, that it is built of bright *and* dark, day *and* night. . . . He must come to grips with the forces of evil, hence the necessity to follow the hidden road of the dolorous quest. His myth . . . is an allegory of self-completion through the mastery and assimilation of conflicting opposites.[6]

Milton would not have found this view wholly uncongenial or strange; he had formulated something like it himself, when he spoke of fallen man.

6 Zimmer, *King and the Corpse,* pp. 34–35.

And perhaps this is that doom which Adam fell into of knowing good and evil; that is to say, of knowing good by evil. And therefore as the state of man now is; what wisdom can there be to choose, what continence to forbear, without the knowledge of evil? He that can apprehend and consider vice with all her baits and seeming pleasures, and yet abstain, and yet distinguish, and yet prefer that which is truly better, he is the true warfaring Christian. . . . Assuredly, we bring not innocence into the world, we bring impurity much rather; that which purifies us is trial, and trial is by what is contrary. That virtue therefore which is but a youngling in the contemplation of evil, . . . and rejects it, is but a blank virtue, not a pure; her whiteness is but an excremental whiteness. . . . Therefore the knowledge and survey of vice is in this world so necessary to the constituting of human virtue, and the scanning of error to the confirmation of truth.[7]

The myth, and the very composition of *Paradise Lost* itself, expresses a recognition, a "coming to grips with" evil. To follow the road of trials, to look on the face of darkness as well as the bright countenance of truth — this was part of Milton's creed. Divergence, as always, arises in the definition of the goal which this process is to achieve. Milton's end is "the constituting of human virtue," and the value of the dark journey hinges on the will, the power "to see and know, and yet abstain." Devoted to the goodness of knowledge as one of his first principles, Milton would have agreed that total self-knowledge is necessary; but necessary for self-discipline. And, since we are by nature impure, a full searching of the dark places was as essential for him as for any modern theorist. He insisted, however, that the descent should be voluntary and deliberate; Satan's knowledge of Hell is not a virtue in itself, though he tries to make it one by inventing the cult of "experience": he taunts Gabriel, as one who "knowst only good, But evil hast not tri'd"

[7] *Areopagitica, SM,* p. 738.

(iv.895–96). Any excursion into the depths must, moreover, be followed by a reascent into the celestial light. Man is not properly defined unless he stands partly in the light, because self-knowledge includes knowledge of our relation to God, which is positive as well as negative. For that, we must ascend as high as the reach of human reason will permit.

Though he included in *Paradise Lost,* therefore, the images of darkness, of underground caves, of hybrid monsters, and of Chaos, Milton arranged them in a pattern that was not their own, being orderly and moral. The mountain-shaped structure alone is evidence of his insistence on the reality of good and evil; in it, moral directions are given physical locations, and the physical itself becomes ethically meaningful. If we fail to see the moral structure of *Paradise Lost,* toward which the myth contributes as the most important of Milton's tools, then we have failed to understand the poem, precisely because moral issues are imbedded in its very texture. Neither images, nor structure, nor dramatic action can be accurately located and described unless they are placed within the ethical frame. If they are so placed, our experience in reading *Paradise Lost* can run parallel to Milton's experience in writing it, which he charted in the prologues to its various books. With him, we can explore the depths and heights, and feel that we have seen and known the span of human experience.

> Thee I re-visit now with bolder wing,
> Escap't the *Stygian* Pool, though long detain'd
> In that obscure sojourn, while in my flight
> Through utter and through middle darkness borne
> With other notes then to th' *Orphean* Lyre
> I sung of *Chaos* and *Eternal Night,*
> Taught by the heav'nly Muse to venture down
> The dark descent, and up to reascend,

Though hard and rare: thee I revisit safe,
And feel thy sovran vital Lamp. (iii.13–21)

Milton did not pretend that understanding is anything but
hard and rare; but as one of his contemporaries wrote, we
cannot have the glory without the hardship. "For all noble
things are as difficult as they are rare."

SELECT BIBLIOGRAPHY

INDEX

SELECT BIBLIOGRAPHY

BIBLIOGRAPHICAL NOTE

I have not attempted to produce here a "complete" bibliography for either Milton studies or researches in myth. Such an undertaking, even if it could be successfully performed, would be inappropriate in a work like this, dealing with only a small area of both fields and emphasizing critical analysis. I have therefore listed only those books to which I can consciously trace some sort of debt, incurred as I was working on the book; the debt is sometimes quite unspecific, and occasionally negative. Any writer will recognize that the construction of such a pedigree is difficult at best, since the literary parents of an idea acknowledged by the conscious mind would often be rejected as step-parents by the unconscious processes that go into the composition even of a critical work. But such as it is, I have made the attempt.

Specifically, the works not included here fall into four categories: general works on Milton which must form the basis of any more particular study (for example, Masson's monumental *Life*); books and articles on specific aspects of Milton that fell wholly outside the scope of this study; writings on myth dealing with particulars similarly remote from my concerns; and finally, the works of Milton's contemporaries and predecessors, to which suitable reference is made in footnotes when they are quoted. The result, as a casual glance will show, is a bibliography composed chiefly of recent works of Milton criticism and scholarship, and a highly eclectic group of books on myth which I happened to find suggestive or informative. It is, therefore, of use only to readers curious about literary genesis, and should not be consulted by those in search of more comprehensive information.

217

Adams, Richard P. "The Archetypal Pattern of Death and Rebirth in Milton's *Lycidas.*" *PMLA,* LXIV (1949), 183–188.

Adams, Robert Martin. *Ikon: John Milton and the Modern Critics.* Ithaca, 1955.

Arthos, John. *The Language of Natural Description in Eighteenth-Century Poetry.* University of Michigan Publications: Language and Literature, XXIV. Ann Arbor, 1949.

Auden, W. H. *The Enchaféd Flood; or, The Romantic Iconography of the Sea.* New York, 1950.

Auerbach, Erich. *Mimesis: The Representation of Reality in Western Literature.* Trans. Willard R. Trask. Princeton, 1953.

Baker, Herschel. *The Wars of Truth: Studies in the Decay of Christian Humanism in the Earlier Seventeenth Century.* Cambridge, Mass., 1952.

Baldwin, Edward C. "Milton and Plato's *Timaeus.*" *PMLA,* XXXV (1920), 210–217.

Barfield, Owen. *Poetic Diction: A Study in Meaning.* London, 1928.

Baring-Gould, Sabine. *Curious Myths of the Middle Ages.* London, 1877.

Barker, Arthur. *Milton and the Puritan Dilemma, 1641–1660.* University of Toronto Department of English, Studies and Texts, I. Toronto, 1942.

——— "Structural Pattern in *Paradise Lost.*" *PQ,* XXVIII (1949), 17–30.

Bateson, F. W. *English Poetry and the English Language.* Oxford, 1934.

Bespaloff, Rachel. *On the Iliad.* Introduction by Hermann Broch. Bollingen Series, IX. New York, 1947.

Blau, Joseph L. *The Christian Interpretation of the Cabala in the Renaissance.* New York, 1944.

Bodkin, Maud. *Archetypal Images in Poetry.* London, 1934.

——— *Studies of Type-Images in Poetry, Religion, and Philosophy.* London, 1951.

Bowra, C. M. *From Virgil to Milton.* London, 1945.

Bridges, Robert. *Collected Essays, II & III.* London, 1928.

——— *Milton's Prosody.* Revised edition. Oxford, 1921.

Brooks, Cleanth. "Milton and the New Criticism." *Sewanee Review,* LIX (1951), 1–22.

Brooks, Cleanth, and John Edward Hardy, editors. *Poems of Mr. John Milton: The 1642 Edition, with Essays in Analysis.* New York, 1952.

Bush, Douglas. *English Literature in the Earlier Seventeenth Century.* Oxford, 1945.

———— *Paradise Lost in Our Time.* Ithaca, 1945.

———— "Recent Criticism of *Paradise Lost.*" *PQ,* XXVIII (1949), 31–43.

Buxton, Charles R. *Prophets of Heaven and Hell.* Cambridge, 1945.

Campbell, Joseph. *The Hero with a Thousand Faces.* Bollingen Series, XVII. New York, 1949.

Carpenter, Rhys. *Folk Tale, Fiction and Saga in the Homeric Epics.* Berkeley and Los Angeles, 1946.

Cassirer, Ernst. *An Essay on Man.* New Haven, 1944.

———— *Language and Myth.* Trans. Susanne Langer. New York, 1953.

———— *Mythical Thought.* Trans. Ralph Manheim. Introductory Note by Charles W. Hendel. New Haven, 1955. (Volume II of *The Philosophy of Symbolic Forms*)

Centeno, Augusto, ed. *The Intent of the Artist.* Princeton, 1941.

Chase, Richard. *Quest for Myth.* Baton Rouge, La., 1949.

Collingwood, R. W. *The Idea of Nature.* Oxford, 1945.

Cornford, Francis Macdonald. *From Religion to Philosophy.* London, 1912.

———— *The Unwritten Philosophy and Other Essays.* Ed. W. K. C. Guthrie. Cambridge, 1950.

Curry, Walter Clyde. "The Genesis of Milton's World." *Anglia,* LXX (1951), 129–149.

———— "Milton's Dual Concept of God as Related to Creation." *SP,* XLVII (1950), 190–210.

———— "Some Travels of Milton's Satan and the Road to Hell." *PQ,* XXXIX (1950), 225–235.

Darbishire, Helen. *Milton's Paradise Lost.* James Bryce Memorial Lecture, 1951. Oxford, 1951.

———— "Milton's Poetic Language." *ESEA* (New Series), X (1957), 31–52.

Diekhoff, John S. "Critical Activity of the Poetic Mind: John Milton." *PMLA,* LV (1940), 748–772.

———— *Milton's Paradise Lost: A Commentary on the Argument.* New York, 1946.

———— "The Trinity Manuscript and the Dictation of *Paradise Lost.*" *PQ,* XXVIII (1949), 44–52.

Dobrée, Bonamy. "Milton and Dryden: A Comparison and Contrast in Poetic Ideas and Poetic Methods." *ELH,* III (1936), 83–100.

Dunbar, H. Flanders. *Symbolism in Medieval Thought.* New Haven, 1929.

Dustoor, P. E. "Legends of Lucifer in Early English and in Milton." *Anglia,* LIV (1930), 213–266.

Eliot, Thomas Stearns. "Milton." *Sewanee Review,* LVI (1948), 185–209.

———— "A Note on the Verse of John Milton." *ESEA,* XXI (1936), 32–40.

Empson, William. *Seven Types of Ambiguity.* London, 1930.

———— *Some Versions of Pastoral.* London, 1935.

Fergusson, Francis. *Dante's Drama of the Mind: A Modern Reading of the Purgatorio.* Princeton, 1953.

Fletcher, Harris Francis. *Milton's Rabbinical Readings.* Urbana, 1930.

Frankfort, Henri, with H. A. Frankfort, John A. Wilson, Thorkild Jacobsen, and William A. Irwin. *The Intellectual Adventure of Ancient Man.* Chicago, 1946.

Frazer, James George. *Folk-lore in the Old Testament.* 3 vols. London, 1918.

———— *The Golden Bough.* One-volume edition. New York, 1945.

Freeman, Rosemary. *English Emblem Books.* London, 1948.

Friedman, Norman. "Imagery: From Sensation to Symbol." *Journal of Aesthetics and Art Criticism,* XII (1953–54), 25–37.

Fromm, Erich. *The Forgotten Language: An Introduction to the Understanding of Dreams, Fairy Tales and Myths.* New York, 1951.

Frye, Northrop. "The Archetypes of Literature." *Kenyon Review,* XIII (1951), 92–110.

———— "Music in Poetry." *UTQ,* XI (1941–42), 167–179.

Gilbert, Allan H. *On the Composition of Paradise Lost.* Chapel Hill, 1947.

Grace, William J. "Orthodoxy and Aesthetic Method in *Paradise*

Lost and *The Divine Comedy.*" *Comparative Literature,* I (1949), 173–187.

Greenlaw, Edwin. "A Better Teacher than Aquinas." *SP,* XIV (1917), 196–217.

―――― "Spenser's Influence on *Paradise Lost.*" *SP,* XVII (1920), 320–359.

Grierson, Herbert J. C. *Milton and Wordsworth: Poets and Prophets.* Cambridge, 1937.

Grimm, Jakob and Wilhelm. *Grimm's Fairy Tales.* Trans. Margaret Hunt. Revised by James Stern. Folkloristic Commentary by Joseph Campbell. New York, 1944.

Haller, William. "Order and Progress in *Paradise Lost.*" *PMLA,* XXXV (1920), 218–225.

―――― *The Rise of Puritanism.* New York, 1938.

Hamilton, G. Rostrevor. *The Tell-Tale Article.* London, 1949.

Hanford, James Holly. "The Chronology of Milton's Private Studies." *PMLA,* XXXVI (1921), 251–314.

―――― "The Dramatic Element in *Paradise Lost.*" *SP,* XIV (1917), 178–195.

―――― "The Evening Star in Milton." *MLN,* XXXVII (1922), 444–445.

―――― "Milton and the Return to Humanism." *SP,* XVI (1919), 126–147.

―――― "The Temptation Motive in Milton." *SP,* XV (1918), 176–194.

Harding, Davis P. *Milton and the Renaissance Ovid.* Illinois Studies in Language and Literature, XXX, No. 4. Urbana, 1946.

Hardy, John Edward. "Lycidas." *Kenyon Review,* VII (1945), 99–113.

Harrison, Jane Ellen. *Ancient Art and Ritual.* London, 1918.

―――― *Prolegomena to the Study of Greek Religion.* Second edition. Cambridge, 1908.

Holmes, Elizabeth. "Some Notes on Milton's Use of Words." *ESEA,* X (1924), 97–121.

Homer. *The Iliad.* Trans. with an Introduction by Richmond Lattimore. Chicago, 1951.

Hooke, Samuel H., ed. *The Labyrinth.* London, 1935.

―――― *Myth and Ritual.* London, 1933.

Hughes, Merritt Y. "The Christ of *Paradise Regained* and

Renaissance Heroic Tradition." *SP,* XXXV (1938), 254–277.
———— "Milton and the Sense of Glory." *PQ,* XXVIII (1949), 107–124.
Huizinga, Johan. *The Waning of the Middle Ages.* London, 1924.
Hulme, T. E. *Speculations: Essays on Humanism and the Philosophy of Art.* Ed. Herbert Read. New York, 1924.
Hunter, William B. "Milton and Thrice-Great Hermes." *JEGP,* XLV (1946), 327–336.
———— "Milton's Materialistic Life Principle." *JEGP,* XLV (1946), 68–76.
Hyman, Stanley Edgar. "Myth, Ritual, and Nonsense." *Kenyon Review,* XI (1949), 455–475.
Johnson, Francis R. *Astronomical Thought in Renaissance England.* Baltimore, 1937.
Jung, Carl Gustav. *Modern Man in Search of a Soul.* Trans. W. S. Dell and C. E. Baynes. New York, 1933.
———— *Psychology and Alchemy.* Trans. R. F. C. Hull. Bollingen Series, XX. New York, 1953. (Volume XII of *The Collected Works of C. G. Jung*)
———— *Psychology and Religion.* New Haven, 1938.
———— *The Psychology of the Unconscious.* Trans. Beatrice M. Hinkle. New York, 1927.
Jung, Carl Gustav, and Károly Kerényi. *Introduction to a Science of Mythology.* London, 1950.
Kelley, Maurice. *This Great Argument: A Study of Milton's De Doctrina Christiana as a Gloss upon Paradise Lost.* Princeton Studies in English, XXII. Princeton, 1941.
Kirkonnell, Watson, ed. *The Celestial Cycle: The Theme of Paradise Lost in World Literature with Translations of the Major Analogues.* Toronto, 1952.
Knight, G. Wilson. *The Burning Oracle.* London, 1930.
———— *Chariot of Wrath: The Message of John Milton to Democracy at War.* London, 1942.
Lang, Andrew. *Myth, Ritual and Religion.* 2 vols., London, 1901.
Langer, Susanne K. *Feeling and Form.* New York, 1953.
Leavis, F. R. *Revaluation: Tradition and Development in English Poetry.* London, 1949.

Lemmi, C. W. *The Classical Deities in Bacon: A Study in Mythological Symbolism.* Baltimore, 1933.

Lévy-Bruhl, Lucien. *How Natives Think.* Trans. Lilian A. Clare. New York, 1926.

Lewis, C. S. *The Allegory of Love: A Study in Medieval Tradition.* Oxford, 1936.

—————— "A Note on *Comus.*" *RES,* VIII (1932), 170–176.

—————— *A Preface to Paradise Lost.* London, 1942.

Lovejoy, A. O. *Essays in the History of Ideas.* Baltimore, 1948.

Lovejoy, A. O., and George Boas. *Primitivism and Related Ideas in Antiquity.* Baltimore, 1935. (Volume I of *A Documentary History of Primitivism and Related Ideas*)

Mahood, M. M. *Poetry and Humanism.* New Haven, 1950.

Malinowski, Bronislaw. *The Foundations of Faith and Morals.* London, 1936.

—————— *Myth in Primitive Psychology.* New York, 1926.

Maritain, Jacques. *The Dream of Descartes.* Trans. Mabelle L. Andison. New York, 1944.

Mayerson, Caroline W. "The Orpheus Image in *Lycidas.*" *PMLA,* LXIV (1949), 189–207.

McColley, Grant. "The Book of Enoch and *Paradise Lost.*" *HTR,* XXXI (1938), 21–39.

—————— "Paradise Lost." *HTR,* XXXII (1939), 181–235.

—————— *Paradise Lost: An Account of its Growth and Major Origins.* Chicago, 1940.

Miles, Josephine. *Major Adjectives in English Poetry.* University of California Publications in English, XII, No. 3. Berkeley, 1946.

Miller, Milton. "*Paradise Lost:* The Double Standard." *UTQ,* XX (1950–51), 183–199.

Murray, Gilbert. *Five Stages of Greek Religion.* Third edition. Boston, 1952.

Nicolson, Marjorie. *The Breaking of the Circle.* Evanston, 1950.

—————— "Milton and Hobbes." *SP,* XXIII (1926), 405–433.

—————— "Milton and the *Conjectura Cabbalistica.*" *PQ,* VI (1927), 1–18.

—————— "Milton and the Telescope." *ELH,* II (1935), 1–32.

—————— "The Spirit World of Milton and More." *SP,* XXII (1925), 433–452.

Panofsky, Erwin. *Studies in Iconology.* New York, 1939.

Parry, Milman. "Studies in the Epic Technique of Oral Verse-Making. I. Homer and Homeric Style." *Harvard Studies in Classical Philology,* XLI (1930), 73–147.

Pope, Elizabeth M. *Paradise Regained: The Tradition and the Poem.* Baltimore, 1947.

Praz, Mario. *Studies in Seventeenth Century Imagery.* 2 vols., London, 1939.

Prince, Frank Templeton. *The Italian Element in Milton's Verse.* Oxford, 1954.

Raglan, Fitz Roy Richard Somerset, Fourth Baron. *The Hero: A Study in Tradition, Myth, and Drama.* The Thinker's Library. London, 1949.

Rajan, Balachandra. *Paradise Lost and the Seventeenth Century Reader.* London, 1947.

—— "Simple, Sensuous and Passionate." *RES,* XXI (1945), 289–301.

Ransom, John Crowe. *The World's Body.* New York, 1938.

Richards, I. A. *The Philosophy of Rhetoric.* New York, 1936.

Robbins, Frank Egleston. *The Hexaemeral Literature: A Study of the Greek and Latin Commentaries on Genesis.* Chicago, 1912.

Ross, Malcolm M. *Milton's Royalism: A Study of the Conflict of Symbolism and Idea in the Poem.* Cornell Studies in English, XXXIV. Ithaca, 1943.

Saurat, Denis. *Blake and Milton.* London, 1935.

—— *Milton, Man and Thinker.* Second Edition. London, 1944.

Seventeenth Century Studies Presented to Sir Herbert Grierson. Oxford, 1938.

Sharp, Robert L. *From Donne to Dryden: The Revolt against Metaphysical Poetry.* Chapel Hill, 1940.

Shumaker, Wayne. "Flowerets and Sounding Seas: A Study in the Affective Structure of *Lycidas.*" *PMLA,* LXVI (1951), 485–494.

Singleton, Charles. "Dante and Myth." *JHI,* X (1949), 482–502.

Stein, Arnold. *Answerable Style: Essays on Paradise Lost.* Minneapolis, 1953.

Still, Colin. *The Timeless Theme.* London, 1936.

Stoll, Elmer Edgar. *From Shakespeare to Joyce.* Garden City, N.Y., 1944.

—— *Poets and Playwrights.* Minneapolis, 1930.

Studies in Shakespeare, Milton and Donne. University of Michigan Publications: Language and Literature, I. New York, 1925.

Svendsen, Kester. "Cosmological Lore in Milton." *ELH,* IX (1942), 198–223.

—— "Epic Address and Reference and the Principle of Decorum in *Paradise Lost.*" *PQ,* XXVIII (1949), 185–206.

Tate, Allen, ed. *The Language of Poetry.* Princeton, 1942.

Taylor, George Coffin. *Milton's Use of Du Bartas.* Cambridge, Mass., 1934.

Thompson, Stith. *Motif–Index of Folk Literature.* Indiana University Studies, XCVI–XCVII, C–CI, CV–CVI, CVIII–CXII. 11 vols., Bloomington, 1932–1936.

Tillyard, E. M. W. *The English Epic and its Background.* London, 1954.

—— *Milton.* London, 1930.

—— *The Miltonic Setting, Past and Present.* Cambridge, 1938.

—— *Studies in Milton.* London, 1951.

Tuve, Rosemond. *Elizabethan and Metaphysical Imagery.* Chicago, 1947.

Waldock, A. J. A. *Paradise Lost and its Critics.* Cambridge, 1947.

Wallerstein, Ruth. *Studies in Seventeenth Century Poetic.* University of Wisconsin [Madison], 1950.

Weisinger, Herbert. *Tragedy and the Paradox of the Fortunate Fall.* London, 1953.

Wellek, René, and Austin Warren. *Theory of Literature.* New York, 1949.

Werblowsky, R. J. Zwi. *Lucifer and Prometheus: A Study of Milton's Satan.* Introduction by C. G. Jung. London, 1952.

Whaler, James. "Animal Simile in *Paradise Lost.*" *PMLA,* XLVII (1932), 534–553.

—— "The Compounding and Distribution of Simile in *Paradise Lost.*" *MP,* XXVIII (1931), 313–327.

—— "Grammatical *Nexus* of the Miltonic Simile." *JEGP,* XXX (1931), 327–334.

———— "The Miltonic Simile." *PMLA,* XLVI (1931), 1034–1074.

Wheelwright, Philip. *The Burning Fountain: A Study in the Language of Symbolism.* Bloomington, Ind., 1954.

Whitehead, Alfred North. *The Concept of Nature.* Cambridge, 1920.

———— *Science and the Modern World.* New York, 1925.

———— *Symbolism: Its Meaning and Effect.* Cambridge, 1928.

Whiting, George W. *Milton's Literary Milieu.* Chapel Hill, 1939.

Willey, Basil. *The Seventeenth Century Background.* London, 1934.

Williams, Arnold. *The Common Expositor: An Account of the Commentaries on Genesis, 1527–1633.* Chapel Hill, 1948.

Wilson, Harold S. "Some Meanings of 'Nature' in Renaissance Literary Theory." *JHI,* II (1941), 430–448.

Wimsatt, W. K., and Monroe Beardsley. "The Intentional Fallacy." *Sewanee Review,* LIV (1946), 468–487.

Wittgenstein, Ludwig. *Tractatus Logico-Philosophicus.* Introduction by Bertrand Russell. London, 1922.

Wölfflin, Heinrich. *Classic Art: An Introduction to the Italian Renaissance.* Trans. Peter and Linda Murray. London, 1952.

Woodhouse, A. S. P. "The Argument of Milton's *Comus.*" *UTQ,* XI (1941–42), 46–71.

———— "Notes on Milton's Views of the Creation: The Initial Phases." *PQ,* XXVIII (1949), 211–236.

———— "Pattern in *Paradise Lost.*" *UTQ,* XXII (1952–53), 109–127.

Wright, B. A. "Masson's Diagram of Milton's Spaces." *RES,* XXI (1945), 42–44.

Zimmer, Heinrich. *The King and the Corpse: Tales of the Soul's Conquest of Evil.* Ed. Joseph Campbell. Bollingen Series, XI. New York, 1947.

INDEX

Abdiel, 106, 185, 190
Academic Exercises, *see* Prolusions
Adam, 18, 142, 186; as Christian
  soldier, 24; vision of future, 31–
  32, 61–62; knowledge, 37–38; as
  ideal man, 66, 97–98; attitude toward Eve, 69; Fall, 79–80, 139, 189;
  ruler of Eden, 153–155; as hero,
  180–181; as Everyman, 205–206
Aquinas, St. Thomas, 37
Areopagitica, 24, 33, 103, 134, 168,
  212
Aristotle, 48, 111, 210
Auerbach, Erich, 52

Bacon, Francis, 11–12, 33 n., 38 n.,
  122
Barfield, Owen, 39 n.
Bateson, F. W., 46
Beelzebub, 152
Belial, 79, 138–139
Bentley, Richard, 76–77, 122
Beowulf, 49
Blackmur, R. P., 5
Blake, William, 31, 38–39, 143, 208–
  209
Bodkin, Maud, 18
Bowra, C. M., 126
Browne, Sir Thomas, 53
Bunyan, John, 21, 184
Bush, Douglas, 161 n.

Cambridge Manuscript, 40, 50, 199 n.
Campbell, Joseph, 23, 195
Cassirer, Ernst, 5, 39, 41, 99, 136 n.,
  145, 169 n., 208
Castiglione, Baldassare, 36–37, 38
Chain of Being, 104, 109

Chaos, 69, 88, 162, 210; as prototype,
  89–91, 135; Milton's description
  of, 104–106, 116–118; after Fall,
  138–139, 168; and Deluge, 176;
  and Satan's voyage, 194–195
Christian Doctrine, 21, 34, 38, 42,
  66, 147, 203
Coleridge, S. T., 48
Comus, 26, 105, 123, 137, 147, 153,
  155–156, 170, 179, 185, 187–189,
  203
Cornford, Francis, 16

Dante, 14, 32, 52, 53, 191–192, 196
Davies, Sir John, 37
*Doctrine and Discipline of Divorce,
  The*, 113, 136–137, 169, 189
Donne, John, 36, 108
Dryden, John, 50, 174–175, 204–205
DuBartas, Guillaume, 13–14, 35, 93,
  110, 115

Eliot, T. S., 1, 96, 208
Empson, William, 149–150, 200
Epic, mythical plots of, 45–46, 49;
  Milton's innovations, 48, 99; chronology of events, 54; diction, 82–
  83, 93–95; similes, 119–120
Eve, dream, 60–61; as ideal woman,
  66; placed below Adam, 69; attitude toward Adam, 77; Fall, 84;
  and pagan goddesses, 121; loss of
  Eden, 191

Fergusson, Francis, 191
Ficino, Marsilio, 33 n.
Fletcher, Giles, 12–13
Frazer, J. G., 9, 10

227